Sacred Pause

*A Creative Retreat for
the Word-Weary Christian*

Rachel G. Hackenberg

PARACLETE PRESS
BREWSTER, MASSACHUSETTS

2014   First Printing
Sacred Pause: A Creative Retreat for the Word-Weary Christian

Copyright © 2014 Rachel G. Hackenberg

ISBN 978-1-61261-579-0

The Paraclete Press name and logo (dove on cross) is a trademark of Paraclete Press, Inc.

Unless otherwise marked, Scripture references are taken from the New Revised Standard Version Bible, copyright 1989, Division of Christian Education of the National Council of the Churches of Christ in the United States of America. Used by permission. All rights reserved.
    Scriptures marked (KJV) are taken from the Authorized King James Version of the Holy Bible.
    Scriptures marked (THE MESSAGE) are taken from THE MESSAGE. Copyright © 1993, 1994, 1995, 1996, 2000, 2001, 2002. Used by permission of NavPress Publishing Group.

PRAYING from the volume THIRST by Mary Oliver, published by Beacon Press, Boston. Copyright © 2006 by Mary Oliver, used herewith by permission of the Charlotte Sheedy Literary Agency, Inc.

Library of Congress Cataloging-in-Publication Data
Hackenberg, Rachel G.
  Sacred pause : a creative retreat for the word-weary Christian / Rachel G. Hackenberg.
     pages cm
  ISBN 978-1-61261-579-0 (hard cover)
  1. Spiritual retreats. 2. Spiritual exercises. I. Title.
  BV5068.R4H33 2014
  269—dc 3   2014020336

10 9 8 7 6 5 4 3 2 1

Published by Paraclete Press
Brewster, Massachusetts
www.paracletepress.com

Printed in China

CONTENTS

INTRODUCTION

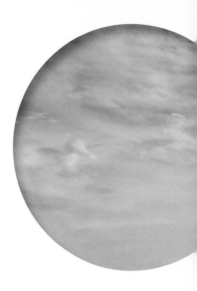

TEN YEARS AGO, my paternal grandfather died. In the years that I knew him, my grandfather—the son of an Old Order Mennonite woman—owned a small farm. "Farm" is a generous word for it. He had a large garden, an acre of cornfield, and an old barn where he raised half a dozen steers for slaughter. When he first bought the property, it was a quiet little place a few miles outside of town. But by the time I was a child sneaking through the house's dusty rooms and swinging with my sisters in the front yard, that small farm was surrounded by suburban development. A modest cul-de-sac neighborhood bordered Grandpa's cornfield, and his bedraggled barn was likely an eyesore to the neighbors. His farm was no longer outside of town—it was very much within the town's suburban expansion.

At my grandfather's funeral service, the minister read those most familiar words of Scripture, "The LORD is my shepherd, I shall not want." Not only did he recite the whole of Psalm 23, but in his homily the minister also meditated on my grandfather's likeness to a shepherd. He told the story that one day a steer got loose from its pasture on Grandpa's farm and Grandpa chased it all through the suburban neighborhood. He labored on foot down the winding street. Around the cul-de-sac. Across a few manicured lawns. Chased down that lost and stubborn steer so he could bring it safely home to the barn, feed it well, and let it rest from its panicked roaming. The minister at the funeral said that—like my grandfather chasing his steer through suburbia—God is a shepherd who chases after us and tends to us.

It was a lovely story to tell, even if it over-romanticized my grandfather's dedication to his small herd of steer. (I'm absolutely certain that Grandpa cursed a blue streak while trying to catch that wandering steer.) Nevertheless the story started me thinking about the image of God as shepherd, about our collective Christian fondness for "The LORD is my shepherd," and about the challenges of bringing an ancient agricultural metaphor to bear in the twenty-first century. When is the last time you or I saw a real-life shepherd, herding real-life sheep, through the hills and the valleys and over the streams of real-life pastures? How many of us have witnessed the daily work of those who maintain the old agrarian ways—watched an Amish boy riding a plow behind two mules, for example, or ridden with cowboys as they herded cattle to auction, or watched children pick tobacco by hand on the family farm—or bent our backs to the same work?

In linguistics, "The LORD is my shepherd" would be said to have *iconic meaning*: the shepherd's activity of sheep-tending represents God's activity of creation-tending. "Shepherd" functions as an icon of "God." A fascinating semantic shift occurs in our religious language—in all language, really—when iconic meaning converts to *coded meaning*, when we no longer distinguish words from their objects. In our faith, for example, Shepherd no longer signifies *God*; Shepherd *is* God. The iconic meaning of shepherd is so consistently recognized in the church that its definition becomes a kind of code, an assumption that functions without explanation . . . and not only without explanation but also without reexamination.

The practice of reexamination is precisely the creative experience that I invite you to attend to here in *Sacred Pause*. Our faith is so full of words, so dependent on words to express itself, that pausing to explore language can deepen and revitalize our faith. Across the pages of this book, we pause to pay attention to the words of Scripture so that we hear the Good News afresh. We pause to see the changes happening to language and to celebrate the transformative impact of words on our faith. We pause to marvel at the Spirit's movement through our sung words, our tweeted words, our blogged words, our Facebooked words. We pause to let words connect us to one another and to the Most Holy God. We pause to explore fresh ways by which the words of faith illuminate the Word itself.

That holy Word, to paraphrase the Letter of James, is the reason for all that we do and the judgment of all that we say. In service to the Word, our words of faith matter. Each time we turn to God in prayer, each time we turn to one another for forgiveness, our words can hinder or advance . . . promise or disappoint . . . encourage or condemn . . . inflame or soothe. Language can draw us closer to God, closer to neighbor, closer to stranger. Words can serve as the vessels of our God encounters.

Yet too often we do not pause to examine what we say, let alone take the time to invest joy and creative energy in appreciating the (sometimes ancient) words of our faith. Instead we often feel inundated by language, struggling to keep up with life and faith in a world that moves at the speed of Twitter feed. But imagine: what fresh perspectives might surprise our spirits when we dust off familiar faith language!

What new meanings we might discover if we pause to peel through the layers of church code! How a renewed curiosity for words might cause us to fall in love anew with the Word!

Linguist Christopher Johnson writes, "We do interesting things when we use language . . . and we should all be able to relish and discuss those things."[1] I've found my own spiritual journey to be reinvigorated by time spent relishing the language of my faith—the words and nuances, the rhymes and stories. *Sacred Pause* is your invitation to approach the words of faith with curiosity, to seek out fuller understandings of our religious vocabulary, to adopt childlike wonder for the sights and sounds and even colors of words, to marvel at the breadth of meaning that words convey, and to make use of words for spiritual renewal and growth.

Here is one example.

Around a blazing bonfire one evening at summer church camp, I distribute red construction paper "flames" to each of my campers, who range in age from nine to twelve. "Write a verb on your paper flame to describe something that fire does," I instruct.

They look puzzled for a moment. "For example, fire burns," I say. "So you might write *burns* on your flame (except now that I used *burns*, you need to find different verbs)." They get the idea and begin to write on their flames.

Verbs finished, we take turns sharing around the circle, using our verbs to create simple sentences.

"Fire burns." That's me, repeating my example.

"Fire warms." The first camper.

"Fire smells." The next camper is waving off smoke.

"Fire destroys."

"Fire brightens."

"Fire explodes."

"Fire cooks."

"Fire melts."

Tossing another log onto our campfire against the cooling evening, I ask the campers to repeat their sentences again, this time replacing *fire* with *God*. They listen and wonder (and giggle occasionally) at each new sentence:

"God burns."

"God warms."

"God smells."

"God destroys."

"God brightens."

"God explodes."

"God cooks."

"God melts."

I can tell from their expressions that my campers are surprised to imagine such divine actions. Does God really cook? What might God melt? How does God smell? Yet our playful exercise captivates their imaginations, and the application of ordinary verbs to the extraordinary God intrigues their spirits. My campfire invitation to explore God through words (sometimes even silly words) suddenly makes God a little more accessible to them, a little more incarnate in their everyday lives. The daunting mystery of "God language" now becomes a delightful curiosity.

The campers' surprise around the campfire reveals their perception of faith words as arcane and abstract, a common impression that resonates across age groups and denominations. Newcomers to churches experience impervious language and irrelevant liturgies as barriers to community. Self-identifying "nones"—that is, those who are "spiritual but not religious"—seek space for holy mystery and imagination far away from tall church steeples. Theologians talk among themselves of eschatology, atonement, and patristics. Denominationalists circle the wagons to examine ecclesiology, hermeneutics, and missiology. Sociologists publish studies on member migration, religious decline, and political corollaries. Meanwhile in the pews, the words of worship say more about who we were than who we are. Too often, our "God language" functions more as a tool of religious institution than a tool of inspiration and connection.

I don't mean to suggest that we can't appreciate the ancient words of our faith histories and of Scripture; I only wonder about all of those coded words that no longer have (or are losing) their cultural connection and significance. How do children make sense of God as Shepherd, returning to Psalm 23 for example, except to memorize it and study an artist's rendering

revitalize your spirit and deepen your faith

of King David in his shepherding days? How do our words facilitate—or encumber—our (re)connection to those who have left the church or to those who grew up without learning Bible stories? How might we find a Living Word from ancient words, both in our collective faith expressions and our personal spiritual lives?

This last question, of course, suggests its own answer: the Living Word itself brings embodiment and understanding to our faith. With confidence in the Incarnate Inspiration, we can pause and observe a creative space in our lives for the Word Made Flesh to spark new words, to inspire imagination, to deepen our faith, to make dynamic use of our tweeted and blogged and texted and Skyped words as vehicles of Good News.

This is why you are here: to revitalize your spirit and deepen your faith. To pause amid all of the words in your life and listen more closely to the Holy Word. To delight once again in your faith vocabulary, in such a creative way that you experience faith itself in new ways. The twelve chapters in *Sacred Pause* provide twelve brief studies of faith language with accompanying creative exercises to guide your reflection.

1. Through "The Sound of Salvation," marvel over the sounds of individual words! Listen closely to syllables, imagine the shapes of vowels, flick consonants from your tongue, and discover the meditative space created by sounds.

2. In "Marching to Zion," engage the rhythms of words, watch them dance and sing, marvel over the colors and smells and emotions evoked by our words, and wonder over the multisensory possibilities they could offer to worship.

3. "The Verb Became Flesh" explores the activity of God in everyday life, much like the campers observing God in action through the flickering flames of a campfire. Bring your creative spirit and a camera phone to this chapter!

4. "The Noun That Is Higher" wrestles with the nouns in our religious vocabulary that function as both the foundations—and the stumbling blocks—of faith.

5. A sense of humor is needed for "Driving Jesus," the chapter that examines the important influence of context on words' meanings. What does a word such as *light* mean in worship, in the Bible, in the aisles of Home Depot, on a yogurt label . . . and how might contextual definitions inform one another?

6. "A World in a Word" expands linguistic context even further through the use of mandalas, the ancient art form that examines the whole of an entity.

7. "Faith Like a Child" asks Why? in its best two-year-old voice, examining assumptions about our religious language, reimagining traditional interpretations, and inviting you to see words and stories from a fresh perspective.

8. "Tipping Sacred Cows" removes the veil of orthodoxy from Scripture and liturgy, and playfully intrudes modern language upon familiar texts in the style of MadLibs.

9. Rest "In the Shadow of Wingdings" in chapter 9, and allow grammar structures to yield to imaginative chaos as you write prayers without form or formula.

10. "Six Words, 140 Characters" dares us to accept the challenge of brevity in our faith talk, exploring the importance of conveying good news concisely to a world of headline-skimmers.

11. In "The Seventh Day," remember the power of rest and silence in language as well as in life. Allow the white space on a page to draw you into a time of literary Sabbath.

12. "How Beautiful the Word" offers a final reflection on the hope and importance of language in faith.

Welcome to this creative space.
Come in, take a spiritual pause—
a deep breath of mind, body, and
soul—and enjoy this retreat.

Your Word is a lamp to my feet
and a light to my path.

Psalm 119:105

The Word became flesh

and lived among us.

John 1:14

I
The Sound of Salvation

....

In the design of the human throat . . .
food has to pass over the trachea
to travel down the esophagus to the
stomach. That makes us more vulnerable
than other animals to choking. This design
flaw emerged in our species because the
configuration enables us to produce a great
range of vocal sounds. We risk choking so
that we can speak.[2]

OMMUNICATION IS THE FOUNDATION
OF COMMUNITIES AND CULTURES.
The coos and clicks, gestures and
expressions that constitute language
enable us to connect with one another, to foster
understanding and cooperation, to give voice to
affection and disagreement, to build alliances or

divisions. With every word, we network our interests and cohere our energies to build towers to the heavens, to raise consciousness and hope, to teach traditions and learn new skills. Words can draw us together or drive us apart, but every time we speak, our throats physically risk choking in pursuit of community. We can be silent, or we can be together. We can embark on faith alone, or we can use our words to reach out to God and to one another along faith's journey.

Many of us have not given a second thought to the coos and clicks, buzzes and hushes—the fundamental articulations of communication—since we last acquired a new language. Perhaps you learned a language in your primary or high school years. Perhaps as an adult you learned a language to prepare for international travel. Perhaps you've not learned a new language since you were a toddler. When studying a new language, the sounds of vowels and consonants are often unique to our ears and peculiar on our tongues, so we practice the sounds by lengthening and repeating them. I remember informal competitions with my friends in high school Spanish class as we tried to outlast one another with our rolled *r*'s: *RRRrrrrrrrrrrthththbb.* The Spanish ñ would have us repeating *Nyeh! Nyeh! Nyeh!* as we learned the sounds of new vocabulary words: *año, jalapeño, ñoñería.*

Once a new language is familiar to our ears and tongues, however, we lose our fascination with its sounds as we accumulate vocabulary, build grammar proficiency, and develop critical-thinking skills within the language. Our curiosity with word sounds wanes as our curiosity with word concepts grows. We make use of words daily, often taking language for granted like the air we breathe and the ground we tread. In faith, too, once we've learned our religious vocabulary, we use words to express faith without giving a second thought to the words themselves. Words are our tool for expressing worship and prayer, for sharing Bible stories and articulating belief.

We learn religious language like we learn any language, slowly acclimating our tongues, our ears, and our minds to these distinct words of faith. Sometimes we learn how to talk about faith from birth; often as adults, we find ourselves relearning faith words as our beliefs mature. In any case, once we learn the religious meanings of words and adopt them into our faith vocabulary, we usually set aside curiosity. Yet the words of faith can be delightful to our ears and spiritual imaginations, if we slow down our lives and our tongues long enough to play with their sounds!

Imagine, for example, if you were hearing the word *spirit* for the first time. Pause for a moment to say it aloud: *spirit*. "Spirit" is a deliciously crisp word with its sounds shaped at the front of our mouths.

● Repeat the word, softly and quickly, listening to its sounds and feeling the word on your lips: *Spirit! Spirit! Spirit!* The sound of *spirit* can be light and quick—not unlike the Holy Spirit's quick help in crisis.

● Say it out loud again, lengthening every sound: *sssssssspppiiiiiiiirrrrriiitttt.* Repeat it again, and hear how the word sounds like a match being scraped across a matchbox until it finally bursts into flame: *sssssssspppiiiiiiiirrrrrIT.* The word's sounds echo our prayer for the Holy Spirit's fire to be kindled within us.

● Now isolate the first consonants of
"spirit" to create a whispering sound:
spspspspspspsp. Let the sounds remind you
of the Spirit's whispering guidance.

Listening to *spirit* was just a warm-up. In order to play with word sounds in such a way as to inspire our spirits, it's helpful to get the whole body involved to practice and improve the connections between mind, body, and soul. Prop open this book, stand up, and follow along.

inspire
our
spirits

Stretch your arms high.

Reach your arms wide.

Stretch your spine down—not too fast! Take your time, breathe deeply, and rise slowly.

Wiggle your toes.

Loosen your tongue by saying: *mah meh mee moh moo.*

Again, but this time exaggerate your jaw movements: *maaah meeeh meee moooh moooooo.*

Push your lips forward and show your teeth. Repeat *t t t t t t t t t t t.*

Wrinkle your nose.

Make a *big* smile.

Stick out your tongue.

Make underwater sounds: *blub blub blub blub blub blub blub.*

Swing your arms high and squeal *whee!* Take your arms and voice even higher, *WHEE!*

Now say *whee!* while grimacing your face and clenching your fists.

Try growling—*ggrrrrrrrr*—while swinging your arms in circles.

Wave your arms high and whisper *sssshhhh.*

Put your finger to your lips and shout *HA!*

Now take a deep breath and pour yourself a glass of water to drink. How did you experience those last four combinations of sound and movement? Why do certain motions seem contradictory to certain sounds? Have you ever noticed what your body does—how its muscles move, what habitual gestures you make, even how your emotions shift—when you speak?

Let's examine this sound-movement partnership briefly. Which sounds seem well-suited to stretching your arms and jaws wide? Open your mouth, reach out your arms, and slowly recite the alphabet aloud, lengthening each letter's sounds. Which vowels and consonants have "open" sounds?

a	*b*	*c*	*d*	*e*	*f*	*g*	*h*	*i*	*j*
	k	*l*	*m*	*n*	*o*	*p*	*q*	*r*	
	s	*t*	*u*	*v*	*w*	*x*	*y*	*z*	

Which sounds correspond with physical tension in your mouth, tongue, and shoulders? Pull up your shoulders, bring your fists close to your mouth, clench your teeth, and repeat the letters' sounds slowly. Which vowels and consonants are articulated best in that closed space? How does the tone of any given letter shift when your body is pulled tightly into itself or relaxed and open?

a *b* *c* *d* *e* *f* *g* *h* *i* *j*

k *l* *m* *n* *o* *p* *q* *r*

s *t* *u* *v* *w* *x* *y* *z*

Now take your time articulating and listening to and playing with sound combinations. For the following list, enunciate the sounds, both quickly and slowly. Listen to your voice as well as to your body. As you repeat the sounds, identify how your body moves to create the sounds, and consider what emotions might accompany those movements.

For example, if *gr* is a sound on the list, make the sound *gggggggrrrrr* and pay attention to the tension in your throat. You might conclude that the emotion of the *gr* sound is stress, because your jaw clenches and your lips barely move to make the sound. If *ch* is a sound on the list, repeat it aloud—*ch ch ch ch ch ch ch.* The sound may remind you of a train, so you might observe that *ch* is a playful sound; or you might notice how your lips purse and how your tongue works constantly and how much air is required to articulate *ch*, so you might conclude that *ch* is a verbal workout!

Try not to skim through the list of sounds. Play with each one as though it is entirely unfamiliar to your ear and tongue. Remember to pay attention both to the motion of your body in producing the sound and to the emotion that accompanies the sound.

gr

ch

tee

ooo

i ("eye")

n

per

hah

sw

oak

um

puh

Massage your cheeks and pour another glass of water if you need one! Feeling silly? Remember, our words—these combinations of vowels and consonants—are our vessel for expressing faith and understanding God. Every letter, every sound, every syllable has the opportunity to spark your connection to the Spirit. Your lips and teeth, tongue and vocal chords, work together to shape the words that just might bring hope to someone today, words that just might communicate your prayers to the ear of God.

spark your connection to the Spirit

In the English language, we're accustomed to representing vowel sounds on paper with these particular shapes: *a, e, i, o, u,* and sometimes *y*. We recognize these shapes as representing the shapes and sounds of consonants: *b, c, d, f, g, h, j, k, l, m, n, p, q, r, s, t, v, w, x, y,* and *z*. The shapes of the alphabet letters on paper cue the ways that our mouths and throats produce the sounds of words.

But the sounds of language are ultimately richer and fuller than twenty-six letters can convey. Our words roll and resonate. They have timbre and color and shape. They rise and fall in pitch, open and close from one syllable to the next. How might we connote the richness of word sounds on paper without using letters? How would we draw the music of language?

When I imagine the sounds of the word *light*, for example—*laaaaahhhheet*—I hear the *aah* rising and expanding slowly like bread dough, with the slightest touch of *t* to cap the word's rising from floating away altogether. The color of *light*'s sounds, to my ear, are warm; not yellow-warm as one might assume from *sunrise* or *lightbulb*, but a warm tan like the color of beach sand. If I were to draw the sounds of *light*, I would draw the expansion of the sounds resonating from the throat and floating like a breath.

Find a set of crayons or colored pencils, and practice drawing word sounds with your own doodles. How would you use color and scribbled shapes to express these sounds?

bō

āhtō

esh

Scribbles on paper remind us of the limits of written language to capture real life, and of the limits of words to fully express faith. Alphabet letters are merely scribbles that represent sounds, and those scribbles have been systematized to become the characters of written language. From an early age we learn that the combinations of letters and sounds into words are still merely representations of real life. When we read the word *water*, for example, we know that the letters and sounds of *w-a-t-e-r* aren't actually H_2O; the word is a written symbol for the liquid that we see and touch in oceans, rivers, raindrops, bathtubs, and sinks. The letters *s-u-n* represent the bright star that warms earth's days, but *s* and *u* and *n* do not compose the sun itself.

When we talk and write and read, we seamlessly connect our words with the real-life objects and events they represent. Not only do we subconsciously translate words into real life, but we also continually translate real life into words. When I see wetness moving through the air, my mind identifies *raindrops*. When I step into a familiar living space, my spirit resonates *home*. As noted in the introduction, we rarely distinguish words as scribbled symbols that are separate from the tangible world. The words and the objects they represent are synonymous for practical purposes. The word *is* the object. The word *is* the action. *L + o + v + e* on paper looks like kindness and care in real life; God's *l + o + v + e* is a tangible experience not limited to letters.

How can we use these exercises to reorient ourselves to the faith words we use so easily—perhaps often, without much thought? To do this, we will try to distinguish the words' sounds from the actions and objects they symbolize, in order to delight in the words themselves. Take *salvation*, for example. The word *salvation* is packed with meaning, and it's one of those religious words that instantaneously calls to mind stories and experiences we've had in the church, both positive and negative. But, if we can separate the word's sounds from its stories, the sounds of *salvation* are soft and smooth, like caramel slowly being stretched: *sssssaaalllvvvvayshun*. The sounds of the word don't rock the boat. They don't have hard edges. You don't have to raise your voice or change your tone to say the word. The sounds are as comfortable as a pillow, as comforting as a layer of Vaseline for chapped lips, as gentle as the colors of dawn warming and shifting before the sun's rise: *sssssaaaalllvvvayshun*.

And—although I indicated that we would distinguish between a word's sounds and its definitions—it's intriguing to notice how the sounds of *salvation* can help our understanding of the word. I know many Christians who have been hurt by a definition of salvation that blazes with damnation. Playing with the word's sounds, hearing its soft sweetness, creates space for remembering the soothing balm of salvation that we can easily miss when we're routinely using (or avoiding) *salvation* in the church. Playing with the sounds of a word can redeem and renew the word!

Following is a list of words from our religious vocabulary, which I invite you to roll around your mouths and tongues and teeth much in the way I just played with the sounds of *salvation*. You might find it helpful to rewrite each word in order to isolate the word's sounds. Play with the word's sounds out loud—slowly, quickly, in separated syllables, with lengthened vowels and repeated consonants. Coo and enunciate as though the word and its sequence of sounds are brand new to you. Manipulate the sounds like toys. There is no right or wrong way to play; your only task is to be curious!

Jesus

Temple

Baptism

Thorn

Ashes

Plowshares

Breath

Flesh

Wisdom

Salt

Fruit

Theologian Robert Beckford notes, "Sound as language is never neutral."[3] The sounds of our words are not merely foundational to our communication of faith; the sounds themselves have the power to convey openness or tension in faith, to encourage or deter love, to inspire or discourage hope. When we pause to savor the sounds of faith words, we dare to risk death (to return to the throat's speech mechanisms) for the sake of giving voice to life.

2
Marching To Zion

Sensory experience is not a plus
to thought, it is the stuff of it. . . .
What we know we know through
our bodies as well as our brains.[4]

*W*E LEARN WORDS THROUGH
EXPERIENCES—not just by
studying consonants and
vowels on paper but by feeling
and living through life. Words are sensual! They have
motion and emotion as we explored in chapter 1, but
more than that, words have energy and color and

rhythm and memory contained within their sounds and definitions. Words dance and convict. Words hint and snap. At their best and fullest use, our words do more than report life; they explode with multidimensional and multisensory life.

It is the rhythm of our communication—pulse, syncopation, pitch—that creates movement between consonants and vowels, within the rise and fall of a sentence, across the arc of a story, through the expression of our prayers. Our lips, teeth, and tongues actually have their own opinions about the rhythmic flow of words, preferring smooth lilts while tripping over uneven rhythms. This is why, for example, we say "salt and pepper" more often than "pepper and salt."[5] Likewise our lips, teeth, and tongues influence our love of reciting Psalm 23 from the King James Version rather than the New Revised Standard Version.

YEA though I WALK through the VALley of the SHAdow of DEATH . . .

In verse 4 of the KJV, the emphasis falls on the first word of every three syllables, like a flowing waltz. (The occasional fourth syllable is inserted into the waltz by syncopation.) In the same verse of the NRSV, the emphasis is irregular, and off-beat.

> *Even though I WALK through the*
> *DARKest VALley . . .*

Does it matter that one version of Psalm 23 has a smoother rhythm than another version? To those who walk, the bumps and curves of a path are minor concerns underfoot, but to those who run (or dance!), the smallest bumps can become a hazard for tripping. The same path is experienced very differently depending on the one traversing it; neither pace is better or worse, but the same bumps affect the runner and the walker and the dancer quite differently.

The bumps—the rhythms—of our words are heard and experienced by our souls quite differently. Consider again the word *spirit*, which we examined in chapter 1. Compare the skip of *spirit*'s two syllables with the yawning single syllable of *god*. Say those words aloud, back and forth: *Spirit . . . GOD . . . Spirit . . . GOD . . . Spirit . . . GOD*. How does the rhythm of *spirit* reflect the Holy Spirit? How does the monosyllabic *god* reflect God? What images, thoughts, and questions are sparked as you compare the rhythms of these two familiar church words? For example, to me the syllables of *spirit* flutter in the wind like a leaf, like the ever-moving Holy Spirit itself. The single syllable of *god* holds steady like a tree trunk, like the constancy of God. A few simple doodles can help us visualize the rhythms we hear.

Spi　　*rit*　　　*God*

Testing out another religious word, the solid and even syllabic rhythm of *discipline* seems to support its meaning.

d　*i*　*sc*　*i*　*pl*　*i*　*ne*

Doodled on paper, the syllables of *discipline* look

- *like mountains: immovable, foundational . . .*
  spiritual discipline builds a faith foundation

- *like a stone skipping across water, its impact rippling*
  beyond itself . . . spiritual discipline affects all areas
  of life

Expanding our attentiveness from rhythm to color, I invite you to reflect: Do words have colors in your mind's eye? Do you dream in color? If God set the world afire in colors, from the golden deserts to the mossy everglades, must our words be limited to two-dimensional black and white?

Pause to wonder, for example: Does *discipline* have a somber hue? What color is the word *light*—in your life experience, in God's imagination? Is *God* a pristine word in cool colors, or a stunning word colored brilliantly like the sunset?

Because the church has already assigned certain colors to certain liturgical seasons, and because language is informed by our senses, we tend to transfer traditional liturgical colors onto words that feature prominently in the corresponding liturgical seasons. *Spirit*, for example, is associated with the season of Pentecost, thus the color of *spirit* is vibrantly red, and it sparks and explodes more like an unpredictable bonfire than a demure altar candle. In the season of Pentecost, *spirit* is the flush of the disciples' excitement as they speak in tongues and preach to the crowds. Then again, *spirit* is also associated with baptism. In the context of baptism, *spirit* flows clear and crisp like a mountain stream; its invigorating presence smells fresh like a spring rain blessing a wheat field. When the Spirit moves through baptism, we watch and listen for the rhythm of water tumbling; we reach out to feel it wet on our fingers. When the Spirit comes at Pentecost, dressed in fiery colors and bursts of sound, we hope to have our own spirits set on fire by the experience of the Spirit's interruption.

Sound and rhythm. Sight and color. Next consider how our sense of touch—along with our memory of touch—is intrinsic to our bodily experience of language. A ball of thick, fuzzy yarn can be described simply as *soft*. Try to imagine a world in which the word *sharp* described all things soft. Would we say *sharp* differently if its meaning were soft? Would we say, "This yarn is shaaaarrrp" instead of "This cactus is sharp!"? Pick up several everyday objects around your home or work or outdoor environment. Hold each object in turn, closing your eyes as you concentrate on the tactile experience. Choose a word to describe how the object feels to touch, and then find an antonym for that descriptive word. Practice saying the antonym aloud as though it is a true description of how the object feels.

The challenge of disassociating our words from our bodily experience highlights the essential multisensory nature of language . . . and of faith. Too often, we are tempted to forget that our words of faith convey real-life experiences—whether our own experiences or the experiences of our forebears. The *wilderness* of ancient Israel's wandering, for example, was a place of dry rocks and fresh streams, of sharp hunger pangs and soft manna. When we repeat the Israelites' story of wilderness, our words (at their best) should remind us that the wilderness was a harsh place for the senses, and our memories should recall those times in our own lives when we have experienced contrasts of dry/fresh, sharp/soft, so that our sensory memories might connect us to the ancient Israelites' experiences. The simple exercise of antonyms reminds us to (re)engage body and language and memory, mind and body and soul.

Let's practice giving attention to our sensory experiences of faith language. Explore the following words slowly, listening and doodling and writing and remembering for each word using these steps:

1. Doodle the syllabic movement of the word, using colors that reflect the sounds of the word.

2. Note the emotion of the word; perhaps add intensity or shade to the word's colors in reflection of its emotional content.

3. What ideas, insights, and questions come to mind as you study your drawing thus far?

4. What memories do you associate with this word?

5. Write down other words from your religious vocabulary that resonate with an emotion similar to this word's emotion.

6. What smells, touches, and other sensory experiences evoke this emotion for you? What sensory experiences and memories from church life evoke this same emotion for you? Be descriptive.

Here's my example of a multisensory reflection on the word *home*.

First I doodle the round sound of oh and the humming base of mmm. I use green, because the sounds are peaceful to my ear, reminding me of the peaceful green pastures of Psalm 23. The shape of my doodle reminds me that home is a centering place with a secure foundation.

From my religious vocabulary, I think of *hope* and *God* as similarly peaceful-sounding words, because they have open vowel sounds. My mind recalls those peaceful times when I've sat in a quiet church sanctuary. I think, too, of my favorite chair, where I can enjoy the afternoon sunlight while reading (or dozing) comfortably.

If you are a worship planner, consider the multisensory experiences that shape your own emotional and spiritual connection to a word . . . and how similar experiences or senses can be engaged in your worship space. How might you take the words of worship beyond the usual audiovisual worship experience into a richer, fuller, more tactile experience? How might words come alive—skip and spark and shine and evoke—not only in worship but also in our everyday experience of God's presence enfleshed in life all around us?

Take your time doodling and reflecting upon the sensory experience of the following words, using the six steps provided on page 48.

Mercy

Lord

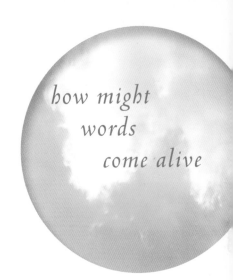

how might
words
come alive

Church

Holy

Fruit

Wind

Love

3
The Verb Became Flesh

T. S. Eliot . . . remarked that it
is the purpose of literature to turn
blood into ink. William Brower was no less
vivid and on target when he said that the
purpose of speaking literature is to turn the
ink back into blood.[6]

ORDS HELP US TELL THE
STORIES OF LIFE AND FAITH
—but more than that, words
actually become part of our lives and our faith. Words,
to borrow from Eliot and Brower, have blood; they
have life. The insights of a deep conversation with
a friend inform your daily living, for example. The

funny joke you read on Facebook lightens your mood. The prayer spoken in worship uplifts your spirit. The words of a newspaper article shape your worldview. The phone call with a family member nurtures the ongoing relationship. Language is not just a life tool; language is a life experience. Our words engage our spirits, minds, and bodies. With every activity in life and faith, our words move and dance and shout and spill and simmer and fall silent. Language functions like a verb in life; it tells what is happening. Often, language itself is part of what is happening. Our experience of life is expressed through verbs.

In the rules of grammar, a sentence is not complete without a verb (the predicate). A noun (the subject) cannot be a sentence on its own; it needs to relate to something, it needs to have action or at least being; it needs a verb. When Moses encounters God in the burning bush, he asks for God's name—a noun—but instead God identifies Godself with a verb, specifically the verb of being: "I AM WHO I AM" or "I AM WHAT I WILL BE." God continues, "Say to the Israelites, 'I AM has sent me to you'" (Exod. 3:13–14). Rather than providing a noun-name, God offers a verb-name—*being*—and

Moses, the ancient Israelites, and we today continue to understand God's being through God's acting: God loving, God satisfying, God rescuing, God revenging, God reconciling, God multiplying, God demanding, God seeking. The being of God is understood through the actions of God; God is understood through verbs.

What are your actions, and how do they demonstrate your being? Make a quick list of ten verbs that you do; focus on everyday activities as well as those activities that bring you joy.

1. _____

2. _____

3. _____

4. _____

5. _____

6. _____

7. _____

8. _____

9. _____

10. _____

Now circle two or three verbs from your list that you think speak to who you are, verbs that reflect your being. Of those two or three verbs, which would you choose as a name for yourself if we, like God speaking to Moses, named ourselves with verbs?

In the days after the resurrection, Jesus calls his friends to lives of verbs.

> Jesus said to Simon Peter, "Simon son of John, do you love me more than these?" He replied, "Yes, Lord, you know that I love you." Jesus said to him, "Feed my lambs." A second time, Jesus said to him, "Simon son of John, do you love me?" Simon Peter answered, "Yes, Lord, you know that I love you." Jesus said to him, "Tend my sheep." A third time, Jesus asked Peter, "Simon son of John, do you love me?" Simon Peter said, "Lord, you know that I love you." Jesus said to him, "Feed my sheep." (John 21:15–17)

Do you love me? Then feed. Do you love me? Then tend. Do you love me? Then feed. Do you love me? Then do verbs.

There are verbs to be done in the name of Jesus that always need to be done: Feed. Tend. Nourish. Care. If you love me, Jesus says, then I will shape and reshape your life for these activities: to feed those who have been neglected and scorned; to tend to the healing of brokenness among your neighbors and your enemies alike. If you love me, Jesus says, then I will call you forward to continue the work that I have left unfinished; you will break bread and you will touch lepers and you will calm storms and you will speak peace.

Feed.

Tend.

Love.

How do these three verbs resonate with you? In what ways are these verbs present (or absent) from the list of ten verbs that you drafted? When you consider the work of Jesus that still needs to be done, what verbs come to mind? What verbs do you feel compelled to participate in with Christ, as part of God's verb-being?

The Gospel of John introduces Jesus as the being of God taking on human flesh and human activity: "The Word became flesh and lived among us" (John 1:14). The Word became an active life that breathed and walked and learned and touched. The Word came out of the abstract being of eternity and entered the tangible circumstances of human life in a particular place and time on earth. And as the Word—Jesus—lived in flesh, those around him saw God's actions in flesh.

The Word became flesh and lived among us.
All things came into being through the Word,
and the Word *was* Being.
And the Word became flesh
and lived
and toddled
and laughed
and cried
and made friends
and learned
and traveled
and ate
and drank
and slept
and gazed at the stars
and watched the sunrise
because the Word became enfleshed.

The Word that is Life *became* a life.
The Word of Being *became* a being.

The Word that is, in fact, the Verb—the holy
Verb that causes Life and Being,
the Verb that is the action of God—
the Verb became flesh
and was born.

And all of the verbs, all of the activities of God
throughout time,
throughout story,
came into flesh:
the creating and the guiding and the
covenanting
and the saving and the anointing and
the judging and the sheltering and the loving,
for the elect and for the foreigner,
for the widow and for the wanderer,
for the king and for the shepherd alike.
All of the activities of God came into flesh in
the Verb that was born of Mary,
the Verb, the sign of God, that was named
Emmanuel: God With Us,
the Verb that was named
Jesus: God heals.

What has come into being through the Verb
is Life:
Life that proclaims "God is here!"
Life that heals the outcast
and comforts the orphan.
Life that makes the leper clean
and lifts up the paralyzed man to walk.
Life that celebrates love
and sets a table for all people.

Life that tells stories
and calls out lifeless and power-driven religion.
Life that transforms
and speaks of new life.
Life that defies death.
Life that is the full glory of God.
Life that beckons our lives to live fully
for God's glory.
Life that radiates Light through the deepest
night and sparks our lights.
Life that is full of verbs.

The Verb became flesh.
The eternal activities of God
took on
Life and Breath and Time
so that our flesh and our breath and our time
could witness to the Verb Made Flesh;
so that all of the daily verbs that we live and do
and say
could reflect the holiness of the Verb's
Incarnation,
could act and live with the courage and the
hope and the trust
that God is made flesh
all around us.

We can practice paying attention to the Verb Made Flesh in the world around us using our cameras and camera phones to take snapshots of everyday life. In the stillness of a photo, actions are captured: something is about to happen, is already occurring, has the potential to take place. A photograph is full of verbs! For your retreat time with the Verb Made Flesh, take some pictures (nothing fancy or staged) or pull out an old photo album. When you view a photograph, allow your mind to wander over the actions (both seen and unseen) captured within the image. Make a list of verbs that might accompany the photograph; you'll need to find a noun with each verb too. Challenge yourself to envision not just what you know about the pictured scene but also what might be unfolding. Try to stretch the range of verbs that your mind applies to the picture in front of you; strive to list ten verbs per picture (and if that's too easy, set a higher goal for yourself). After you've listed your action verbs, do as my campers did in the introduction and attribute those verbs to God!

I've provided some everyday images on the following pages to get you started.

4
The Noun That Is Higher

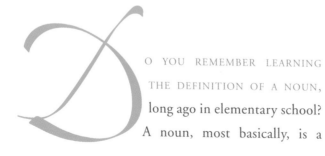

A case of contradictories, both of
them true.
There is a God. There is no God.
Where is the problem? I am quite sure that
there is a God in the sense that I am
sure my love is no illusion. I am quite sure
there is no God, in the sense that I am sure
there is nothing which resembles what
I can conceive when I say that word.[7]

O YOU REMEMBER LEARNING
THE DEFINITION OF A NOUN,
long ago in elementary school?
A noun, most basically, is a

word that identifies a person, place, or thing. Nouns are concrete by nature. They identify a specific being, a specific object, a specific event, even a specific idea. Although nouns can have many definitions, as we will explore in chapters 5 and 6, nouns are not known for being abstract. They can be pinpointed on a map or timeline; their elements can be examined and their themes outlined.

I remember a poster from my teenage years in the church titled "And He Shall Be Called . . ." The poster lists fifty-plus names for Jesus Christ based on images of God from the books of the Bible: Advocate, Dayspring, High Priest, Good Shepherd, True Vine, Bright Morning Star, and so on. Many of these are familiar names, venerated names, beloved names . . . and nouns, every one of them. Nouns as names for Jesus and God strive to label who the divine is. Nouns strive to make the mystery of God concrete, but in doing so, nouns for God cause two problems. First, as Simone Weil observes, the moment we imagine God within the boundaries of a noun, God outmaneuvers and escapes our conceptions. The moment we name God as *Vine*, for example, God surprises us and becomes the branch, the root, the bloom, or even (to use a new definition of *vine*) a short stream of videos. Second, as I noted in the introduction, names for God function as symbols—codes into which we embed our assumptions and stories. Coded names (nouns) for God require inside knowledge of religious life and teachings. *True Vine*, for example, requires a knowledge of John 15.

Ironically, the use of nouns to concretize God's identity in our faith actually introduces a new mystery: the church code. Church codes assume familiarity with the particular culture of a congregation, denomination, or religious practice. When God is named Rock in church settings, without explanation or elaboration, the church code assumes a familiarity with Psalm 18. The encoded meaning of *Rock* is the image of God as the unmovable foundation of our lives no matter life's changes. When *Rock* is used as God's name, the church code does not intend to convey that God is loud and rhythmic and drives the dance of the universe like a rock and roll band. Nor does the church code of *God our Rock* imply that Christians experience God like crack cocaine! When we use *Rock* as a noun-name for God, the word comes encoded with a particular definition; the code expresses a concrete image for God that has very particular parameters . . . and we assume that everyone else in Christianity uses the same code, without any need for explanation.

Of course, names of God are not the only noun-codes within our faith vocabulary. Many words have assumed meanings: words like *salvation, cross,* and *creation* are not only used to tell the story of God's work but also, in some settings, to hint at a whole set of beliefs. When I studied in seminary, such nouns were great fodder for classroom debate. "What is the nature of *salvation*? What distinguishes a *sacrament* from a *rite*? What is the role of *pastor*? How is the *cross* defined?" Churches today find themselves struggling and stressed over nouns like *leadership, growth, budget,* and *vision.* Where have you heard nouns debated among people of faith? What are the noun-names for God that you particularly love?

By their definitive nature, nouns have the possibility of being foundations of our faith or stumbling blocks to it. Often the very same nouns function in both capacities! When we pause to listen closely to the nouns that we use in worship and prayer and conversation, we can (re)discover their meanings and develop new appreciation of these vital words of faith. We can also, as a result of listening to the words, find new ways to talk to each other about our faith so as to avoid setting stumbling blocks in front of one another.

find new ways to talk to each other about our faith

Because we know, from our own lives and church experiences, sometimes we trip or even block each other as we strive to define faith. I wonder, sometimes, if we are perhaps so eager for a word—for any word to draw us closer to the Word—that we set words in stone in order to feel secure in our understanding. Yet as soon as our words become stones, as soon as they become encoded nouns, they fail to have the fullness of life that we explored in chapters 1–3. If and when, however, we attend to the nuance and richness of our nouns, when we engage our words rather than idolizing them, we respect the mystery that is the Word beyond objectification.

Ultimate Being,

Spectacular Beyond,

you are

maybe

kinda

sorta

like the breath

that inflates my lungs

and reminds my body of peace.

Creative Animation,

Profound Revelation,

you are

maybe

kinda

sorta

like the tree

that extends beyond my vision

and reveals faithfulness that remains through life's

seasons.

Delightful Abstract,

Surprising Particularity,

you are

maybe

kinda

sorta

like the smile

that renews my soul

and draws me beyond myself.

Allow me to offer one example of decoding a "sacred noun" in such a way as to strengthen our faith foundations through fresh examination: "Come to me, all you that are weary and are carrying heaven burdens, and I will give you rest. Take my yoke upon you, and learn from me; for I am gentle and humble in heart, and you will find rest for your souls. For my yoke is easy, and my burden is light" (Matt. 11:28–30).

I suspect that only a few of us can give testimony to the experience of watching a pair of large oxen or sturdy mules lumbering across a large, rolling field, tilling the ground in preparation for its planting, with a heavy wooden yoke padded with leather lying across the necks of both animals, pulling behind them an ancient farming instrument with long metal tines dragging through the earth, and a young Amish or Old Order Mennonite man with a straw hat perched and riding above the rolling tines. The yoke—familiar to Jesus' audience in his day, familiar to agrarian communities for the centuries before the Industrial Revolution, familiar to agricultural communities that still practice Old World farming methods—is otherwise an outdated image in these modernized times. "Take my yoke upon you" is a sacred saying in church life and the yoke is an encoded symbol that conveys spiritual reprieve; despite its familiarity to our faith, "yoke" is distant from our everyday lives and thus remains a religious cliché lacking depth of meaning and relevance.

But see if this image is familiar to you: I have two children who are growing in leaps and bounds. Because they are growing so fast, I refuse to buy expensive shoes that will be outgrown by the end of a season. Consequently, every four or six months we go shopping in that cute little boutique known as Targét. When you shop for shoes in a store like Target, you have to tolerate the little tags and white elastic strings that are used to keep shoes together amid the chaos of a box store's shoe department. On any given shoe-shopping trip, I tie a new pair of sneakers onto my son's or my daughter's feet and say, "Walk up and down the aisle for me, and see how they feel." So my kids walk down the shoe aisle like awkward ducks, taking short strides with that elastic string still holding the shoes together.

Jesus said, "Take my yoke upon you. Tie yourself to me. Be bound to me like one shoe is bound to its match, like one ox is bound to its partner by a yoke, so that the two are never separated. Walk in step with me. Synchronize yourself to my ways. Coordinate your life with mine. And whatever burdens you are carrying, whatever weight you pull behind you, we will hold that burden together as two who are so inherently familiar with one another that they walk in step . . . and together, your burden will be made light.

"Together, this yoking —

this tying-together —

this walking-together

and working together

will be made easy,

and I will truly give you rest."

Once decoded, the "yoke" takes on fresh meaning for faith. With examination, "take my yoke upon you" becomes more than a cliché; it becomes an actual invitation to be bound anew to Christ, to fall into step with the One who can relieve and delight our lives.

Following is a list of nouns for your examination and reflection. With each, consider the ways in which the word may pose a stumbling block to faith (e.g., lack of contemporary context, as with "yoke") and the ways in which the word may inform our faith foundations. I've jotted some notes on the first noun to get you started.

| *Noun as Foundation* | *Noun as Stumbling Block* |

GATE (John 10:1–9)

| *Christ-the-Gate as a point of access, swinging open in invitation* | *Christ-the-Gate as gatekeeper, imposing and preventative* |

Christ-the-Gate creating a safe pasture for all sheep to graze

OFFERING (Mk. 12:41–44)

| *Noun as Foundation* | *Noun as Stumbling Block* |

SALVATION (Phil. 2:12–13)

LORD (Matt. 7:21–23)

| *Noun as Foundation* | *Noun as Stumbling Block* |

FLESH (John 6:56)

SIN (Lk. 11:4)

5
Driving
Jesus

Social media expert Stowe Boyd
wrote in his blog, "I have found
myself reading less in recent years:
reading in the sense of hours immersed
in a book, curled up on the couch. I
am reading more today, in terms of text
passing through my eyes, than ever before,
however. It's just time spent in the browser."
Although there's some debate as to whether
we're actually reading less, no one denies
that we're reading differently.[8]

LANGUAGE IS CHANGING, AND
HOW WE USE LANGUAGE
IS CHANGING. We skim
and scroll, browse and
download. We invent new

words, and we use old words in new ways: from the expanding definitions of words like *twitter*, *hack*, *stream*, and *mouse* to the total invention of words like *muggle*, *swag*, and *fracking*. Our grammar and spelling are changing too, thanks in no small part to text messaging and instant messaging; *ur* substitutes for both *your* and *you're*, and we use emoticons rather than words to express how we feel.

But language is just one of many changes we are experiencing. Life is new at every turn: we change jobs and relocate; our families grow and decrease; our faith deepens; our worldviews change; we struggle and we soar with each new life stage. Some bemoan life's changes, others celebrate them, but change itself is actually neutral. How we respond to the shifting tides creates the positive or negative value of change. Besides, "despite our apprehensions, without change we could scarcely know anything at all."[9] Change is critical to our understanding of the world and to our growth in faith.

Scripture helps us meet change with a welcoming spirit. Story upon biblical story reminds us that the unchanging God meets us faithfully in new and changing circumstances, giving us new understanding of ancient faith. If we follow the story of *covenant* across the Old Testament, for example, we can discover that even such a foundational theme of faith can be given new expressions as time passes and life alters:

from God's covenant with Noah, displayed in the rainbow, in which God promises to no longer be a warring god;

through the covenant with Abraham, in which God and Abraham publicly claim one another— "I will be your God and you will be my people"— with a promise to Abraham of land, children, and a reputation as the ancestor of a new nation;

the continued covenant written in stone for Moses and the wandering Israelites after their escape from slavery in Egypt, because the people are no longer a small tribal family but a nomadic multitude who need to live in covenant not just with God but also now with one another in order to survive in that wilderness;

and into the years of exile, during which the beloved temple in Jerusalem—the central image of God's covenant—is destroyed by the conquering Babylonians. In those days of exile, as the people struggle to survive from one day to the next, their faith struggles to survive as well: how do you continue to trust in God's covenant if you don't have the homeland that Abraham longed for, if you don't have the temple that was imagined by refugees in the wilderness, if you don't have your community to remind you of God's laws and blessings?

The prophets, too, struggle to understand God's covenant in light of the exile. The prophet Jeremiah knows the difficulty of holding on to faith, yet he preaches the reliability of God's covenant. "Again I will build you, and you shall be built, O Israel. Again you shall take your tambourines and dance, again you shall plant vineyards on the mountains of Samaria. Again I will be the God of all the families of Israel, and they shall be my people . . . and I will make a new covenant with the house of Israel and Judah; I will redefine it, and it will not be like the covenant that I made with their ancestors" (Jer. 31:4–5, 1, 31–34, adapted).

Through Jeremiah, God promises that the covenant will be renewed and reimagined for the exiles returning home. No longer will the covenant look like a husband (Jer. 31:32) providing the security of a home and a name to his wife, as God first promised to Abraham and then to the Israelites who wandered with Moses. No longer will the covenant look like a teacher (Jer. 31:34) enforcing the rules of behavior on irresponsible students, as it did when God gave ten commandments to Moses or sent snakes to correct the people's complaining. In that moment, in those days of bitterness and exile, it's as though God assesses the whole scope of the covenant and determines that it needs a significant update:

God looks back at Noah and sees that the covenant given to one man in a boat cannot meet all of the needs of a nation in exile;

God looks at Moses and sees that the stone tablets given on a mountain were too easily broken and the bronze snake draped on a pole was too easily idolized—that tangible symbols for the covenant are limited in their usefulness;

God looks at the whole history of giving the people a concrete covenant that they could touch in stone or account for in acreage; a concrete covenant that could be maintained by memorizing rules and Scripture verses, by the faithful practice of temple sacrifices and weekly worship; and God sees that the concrete covenant of blessings and curses, rules and rituals is no longer enough. The world of empires and exiles has become more complicated; the covenant needs to be experienced by and embodied within the people themselves.

So when, in the days of Jeremiah, God hears the people in exile lamenting, "Where is God's covenant? How can we know that God is with us without our temple? How can we experience God's covenant when we're not in our homeland?" God vows, "I will bring you home again, and when you get home, there will be a new covenant—*you* will be the new covenant. Each of you will have my covenant within you. Each of you will know that I am your God and you are mine. Each of you will be responsible for nurturing this covenant with me and with one another. You yourselves will bring the covenant to life from where it is written on your hearts, so that when people see you, they see my covenant.

"My covenant within you will become a catalyst. No longer does this world need a covenant carved in stone—it needs a covenant embodied in flesh that will get up and move about and seek to gather in the blind and the lame, the elders and the young women with children, the widows and the proud kings, gathered from all corners of the earth (Jer. 31:8) so that I can love them. With my covenant written on your hearts, this will be your task—to embody my goodness to all people, for the sake of the healing of all nations. My covenant on your hearts will be a catalyst. I will make you my stewards for the work of restoration, for the work of change."

God reimagines the covenant, gives it flesh, and gives the people a new understanding of it. What the people cannot imagine—a covenant without stones, brick, and mortar—God imagines in the people themselves, just as God once imagined rescue for Noah when flood waters rose, just as God imagined family for Abraham when he was childless, just as God imagined home for escaped slaves on the run from Egypt, just as God imagined restoration to those living in exile.

When the ancient Israelites' lives changed across generations, God reshaped the covenant so that each generation could understand the covenant anew. Change is the opportunity for new understanding and reimagining in faith. When our lives shift, we necessarily reexamine who we are and how we live.

Often our words can clue us in to the changes we are experiencing. (Sometimes the words represent the changes themselves.) When we listen—creatively, playfully—to our words amid life's changes, a sacred space for reimagination is created and our spirits can find fresh understanding. Take this sentence from Mark 1:12, for example: "The Spirit immediately drove [Jesus] into the wilderness." For years, I've read this verse and wondered with a chuckle, "What kind of car did the Spirit use to drive Jesus into the wilderness? Was it a nice car for the Son of God? A fast and fancy car?" Surely the Gospel writer would not have meant to suggest the use of an automobile in this story; the meaning of *drive* has changed greatly over the centuries! No doubt it's more fitting to understand *drove* in Mark to be akin to driving sheep or cattle . . . but that, in turn, raises new questions: if the Spirit herded Jesus into the wilderness, should we infer that Jesus resisted going there or that he would have strayed without the Spirit's guidance? Did the Spirit drive Jesus with the intensity of a jockey whipping his horse in a race? Is a certain speed and intensity implied by *drive*, as though the Spirit was in a hurry for Jesus to meet temptation?

When we listen to the ways in which *drive* is used today, after centuries of technological change in our world, and we intrude our modern definition on the ancient context of Mark 1, a new and rather silly story emerges! While such foolishness may seem trivial, this bit of wordplay challenges us to linger over the Bible verse and to read it differently. Out of the image of Jesus and the Spirit cruising in a Ford Mustang, we can find surprising questions to take into a retreat for reflection: Do I experience the Spirit as a friendly traveling companion or as an unrelenting herder? How does the Spirit send me into the wilderness . . . and how do I resist or enjoy the journey there?

Though we tend to treat religious language as though it is impervious to context and unchanged by time, the opportunity to let words help our spirits respond to life's changes with curiosity and courage is an important exercise in faith. For you to meet change with a spirit of faith and creativity, I've clustered together Bible verses that share a common word, but I've replaced that shared word with a blank space. As you read the verses in their clusters, brainstorm various words that might be suitable for each set of verses. You're not looking for one "right" word (although it's likely that you'll figure out the word shared by the verses); instead imagine *how many words* suit the context of each set of verses. If you only come up with one or two words, explore synonyms to find additional words. As you fill in the blanks, attune your spirit to the meanings of the verses as they shift with each new word, just as the ancient Israelites experienced "covenant" differently with each new context. What fresh insights are revealed by the changes?

"You give the gift of a _____ always,

and you make me glad with the joy of your presence,

O God!" (PS. 21:6, ADAPTED)

•

"God said to Abram, 'I will make you great among the

nations and your name will be known, so that you will be

a _____ to all people.'" (GEN. 12:2, ADAPTED)

•

"The LORD said, 'I am setting before you today the choice

between a _____ and a curse, to determine

whether God will be with you in the fight ahead."

(DEUT. 11:26, ADAPTED)

•

"Who knows, but perhaps God will turn back toward you

and leave a _____?" (JOEL 2:14, ADAPTED)

•

"The disciples were full of joy and continually in the

temple _____ God."

(LK. 24:52–53, ADAPTED)

"The LORD your God travels along with your camp, to

_____ *you from your enemies*

and to give you victory over them." (DEUT. 23:14, ADAPTED)

•

"Be a hiding place for me, a strong castle

to _____ *me."* (PS. 31:2, ADAPTED)

•

"Listen to me: I carried you at your birth and now in your

old age I carry you again. I will hold you up and I will

_____ *you."* (ISA. 46:3–4, ADAPTED)

•

"When Peter noticed the strong wind, he was scared and

began to sink into the water; and he cried out,

'Jesus _____ *me!'"* (MATT. 14:30, ADAPTED)

•

"We all growl like bears and mourn like doves. We are

waiting for justice, but there is none. We are waiting for

someone to _____ *us, but nothing happens."*

(ISA. 59:11, ADAPTED)

"These are but the merest hints of his ways! How small a whisper do we hear and understand! But the thunder of God's _____, who can comprehend it?"

(JOB 26:14, ADAPTED)

•

"Your right hand, O LORD, glorious in _____, shattered the enemy." (EXOD. 15:6, ADAPTED)

•

"Stay here in the city, until you have been clothed with _____ from on high." (LK. 24:49, ADAPTED)

•

"Is the LORD's _____ limited? Now you shall see whether my word will come true for you or not."

(NUM. 11:23, ADAPTED)

•

"They forgot God's _____; they did not remember the day when God rescued them."

(PS. 78:42, ADAPTED)

"Before the _____ were born, before you had formed the earth and the world, from everlasting to everlasting you are God." (Ps. 90:2, ADAPTED)

•

"Come up to me on the _____ and wait there." (Exod. 24:12, ADAPTED)

"Climb a high _____ to herald the good news; lift up your voice with strength; say to the people, 'Here is your God!'" (Isa. 40:9, ADAPTED)

•

"The _____ quaked before the LORD, the One of Sinai, the God of Israel." (JUDG. 5:5, ADAPTED)

•

"You will say to the _____, 'Move from here to there,' and it will move." (MATT. 17:20, ADAPTED)

"Have regard for your _____, for the dark

places of the land are full of the haunts of violence."

(PS. 74:20, ADAPTED)

•

"I will remember my _____ that is between

me and you and every living creature of all flesh."

(GEN. 9:15, ADAPTED)

•

"Therefore the people observed the sabbath throughout

their generations, as a perpetual _____."

(EXOD. 31:16, ADAPTED)

•

"Then Jonathan made a _____ with David,

because he loved him as his own soul."

(1 SAM. 18:3, ADAPTED)

•

"I have taken you by the hand and kept you; I have given

you as a _____ to the people."

(ISA. 42:6, ADAPTED)

6
A World in a Word

The distinction between
denotation [an informational
definition] and connotation
[subjective mental associations] is fine
as far as it goes—but it doesn't go very far.
If you think of meaning as a network, you
see how it can go off in different directions
from the same point of origin.[10]

THANKSGIVING.

What comes to mind for
you, simply by my mention of
the word *thanksgiving*?

What are the smells, sounds, and stories that flood your memory if I capitalize the word *Thanksgiving*?

How do you define *thanksgiving*?

What is the mood of *thanksgiving*?

We can list multiple meanings for *thanksgiving*, we can tell many diverse stories about *Thanksgiving*, and all of those different definitions, synonyms, stories, sights and smells are connected as a network by twelve simple letters: *t-h-a-n-k-s-g-i-v-i-n-g*. That network, in turn, links to other networks of words and people and stories and places; for example, the memory of my mother's fudge pie at Thanksgiving reminds me that I need to buy cocoa at the grocery store to make that same pie for tomorrow's company picnic. It's like a game of Six Degrees of Separation, in which we discover that two seemingly unrelated people can, through a series of relationships, discover that they share something in common. Or it's like visiting a new church and remembering that, despite some stylistic and theological differences, we share Christ. "The networks around us are not just webs. They are very dense networks from which nothing can escape and within which every node is navigable. This is why there are no islands of people completely isolated from society at large and why all molecules in our body are integrated into a single complex cellular map."[11]

In our highly interconnected world of relationships and faith, we can meditate on one single word—with its links and references and stories and associations—until that one word connects to a whole world of meanings, even to the whole world itself. Let's take a snapshot of the world contained within the word *thanksgiving*.

Thanksgiving is a compound word, *thanks* + *giving*. By definition, thanksgiving is a verb that means "to show or to offer thanks." Within the United States, this same word is a noun that names a November holiday. A flurry of cultural images and activities rushes to mind in conjunction with Thanksgiving based on American history, folklore, and holiday advertisement: a turkey feast, family gatherings, television-watching, post-holiday shopping, elementary school dramas featuring be-feathered Native Americans and hatted Pilgrims eating popcorn together. Many of us can recall the particular foods and smells of our families' Thanksgiving tables. We have stories about Thanksgivings that went poorly, or we have traditions we've created to counter the "traditional" Thanksgiving event. Personally, when I think of the Thanksgiving holiday, I hear Perry Como singing "Oh there's no place like home for the holidays."

This whole world of images, stories and experiences, sights and sounds, exists in and around the word *thanksgiving*—and I haven't even mentioned the significance of the word in church life! *Thanksgiving* is present in our methods of weekly offering, in our Sunday hymns, in our church fund-raising campaigns, in our ecumenical and interfaith celebrations, in our hunger-related mission efforts! Whether we realize it or not, an entire networked world is present every time we read the word *thanksgiving*.

Since ancient times, the mandala has served as a circular representation of whole worlds, entire entities. The mandala may artfully symbolize the whole of the cosmos, the whole of a person's life, the whole of a story, the whole hierarchy of gods, for example. In many places and across religions, the mandala is used not only to represent a whole system but also to meditate on and seek its center—its core value. One common mandala used in churches today is the labyrinth, the paths of which a person may walk (or trace by finger) while reflecting on the whole of one's life or seeking one's center. Stained-glass rose windows are another example of beautiful mandalas in the Christian tradition.

Of course, the mandala is not unique to Christian symbolism. One peer of the mandala is the yin and yang symbol of Taoism; the yin and yang represents the universe with its "dynamic system . . . of opposing and complementary forces."[12] In the yin and yang, polarities are affirmed and held together within the whole: darkness cannot be seen without light, aggression does not exist without retreat, what is definite cannot be understood without mystery. Every time we try to take a singular perspective, the yin and yang symbol requires us to see the whole.[13]

The yin and yang symbol and the ancient mandala call us to remember the whole networked world when we encounter a single word: to pay attention to context, to be mindful of nuance, to welcome the complexity of a fuller picture. If we are honest, we are not adept at seeing the whole of a word—let alone the whole of the world. Our daily habits confine us to particular definitions and worldviews. Our short-term memories are selective. Our egos are self-serving. It's not easy to nurture a holistic mindfulness of our words and our faith; we have trouble gaining clarity on just *one part* of the whole.

The Letter of James provides a helpful analogy to challenge us beyond our limited vision and our fleeting attention spans. "For if any are hearers of the word and not doers, they are like those who look at themselves in the mirror; for they look at themselves and, on going away, immediately forget what they were like" (Jas. 1:23–24). How many of us have had the experience of looking in a mirror, checking ourselves over, walking away . . . and then returning to the mirror because we can't remember if we combed our hair or straightened our tie or put on makeup? Perhaps you've had the experience of checking yourself in the mirror and then going about your day, only to realize later that you missed noticing in the mirror that you were wearing two different shoes, forgot to put on earrings, or left a zipper down!

According to James, just as we look in the mirror and forget what we've seen, sometimes we hear lessons of faith or we read words of faith or we sing our declarations of faith . . . but we forget to put faith into practice. We fail to take the words and do what they say. We see part of the whole—the words and lessons of faith—but we forget to see the entire picture—how it applies to our lives. We fail to show what we believe.

We say "Do unto others," but we snap at the grocery store clerk or at the neighbor.

We say "Love everyone," but we're suspicious of anyone who lives in an unfamiliar part of town.

We say "God is grace," but we can't forgive our own imperfections and we hold grudges against others.

We hear the words of faith, but we fail to live consistently with faith.

We look in the mirror, but we forget what we've seen.

James is simple and direct in his challenge: Are we living out our faith, or are we just giving it lip service? James not only admonishes us not to look in the mirror and forget what we've seen, but he also challenges us not to look in the mirror and only see part of the image reflected there. We've got to look in the mirror from head to toe! We must embody faith in every aspect of our lives! If we read the entire Letter of James, we hear him addressing the whole breadth of our lives:

our impulses for instant gratification,

our envy of wealth,

our lack of care for those less fortunate,

our gossiping,

our hypocrisy and double-standards,

our relationships,

our egos!

Do we examine the practice of faith in our lives from head to toe . . . or do we only look at one aspect of faith, at one part of our lives—only our Sundays and not our weekdays, for example, or only our prayed words and not our Facebook words? How are our relationships showing our faith? How are our words showing our faith? How are our finances showing our faith? How are our daily activities, our work, our church work, our hobbies, our time, and our volunteering all showing our faith?

And one step further: not only is the mirror a tool for seeing the whole of ourselves (actually as well as metaphorically), but it can also be used to reveal the world beyond us. In James 1:25, the challenge to our breadth of perspective continues:

"Whoever catches a glimpse of the revealed counsel of God—the free life!—even out of the corner of his eye, and sticks with it, is no distracted scatterbrain but a person of action who finds delight in doing." (THE MESSAGE)

Do you have a mirror nearby? Stand in front of it or hold it in front of you. Take a look. You see yourself in the mirror, of course; even a small hand mirror can be tilted to look yourself over from head to toe. James has been clear that we need to see the whole picture of ourselves, to pay attention to faith in every part of our lives. With verse 25, James instructs us to take a few steps back from the mirror (or to tilt the mirror from side to side) in order to see more than ourselves in the mirror's reflection. Those who consistently put faith into action, James writes, are the ones who look into a mirror and don't see only themselves: they also see God and they see others. They not only pay attention to the whole image of themselves but also try to gain perspective on the whole world. The life of faith is about love of God and love of neighbor, and we can't see or love God and neighbor if we keep the mirror right in front of our own faces!

Seeing beyond ourselves to the big picture—looking beyond the part to the whole—is perhaps the hardest and certainly one of the most consistent challenges of faith! We experience life in the first person. We are always inside our own heads. When we have good news, we want the focus to be on us; when we experience pain, we want the focus to be on us. Attention feels good—we even want God's focus to be on us! James moves the mirror away from us and challenges us to gain perspective on the whole.

With our retreat time in this chapter, we heed James's encouragement to tilt the mirror and find a broader perspective on the whole, using words to trace the networks into the world. Now we want to go beyond definitions and synonyms to the vast world of experiences that we connect to our words. To do this, we can create mandalas that are centered on words; we can fill in and flesh out the whole world of a word using the circular mandala form. We can artistically reflect on the biblical context of a word, its church definitions, and also comb through a word's implications, innuendos, cultural contexts, song memories, stories, and so on.

Let me offer an example of a word mandala using the word that I considered at the outset of this chapter: *thanksgiving*.

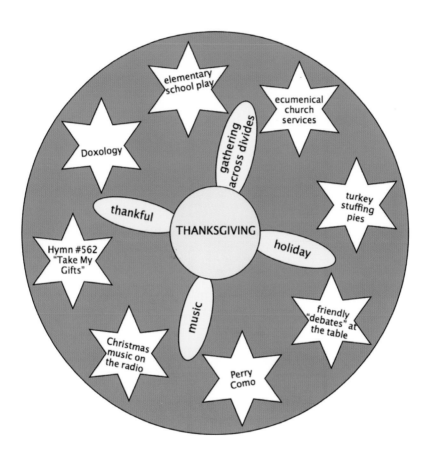

You are invited to draw and write and color as you reflect upon the whole world of a word: its definition(s) and stories, its nuances and histories, your own life experiences of the word, the senses and emotions of the word, even the sound-alike or look-alike words that come to mind when you see the word. Think about music, Scripture, songs, even rhyming words. Think about what a word means to your faith and how you respond to it emotionally. The following mandalas are available for your focus and reflection. Fill in each mandala slowly around its central word. Use color if you would like. These mandalas have been drafted with basic geometric designs; you may want and need to enhance the design to make room for the cosmos that you're representing.

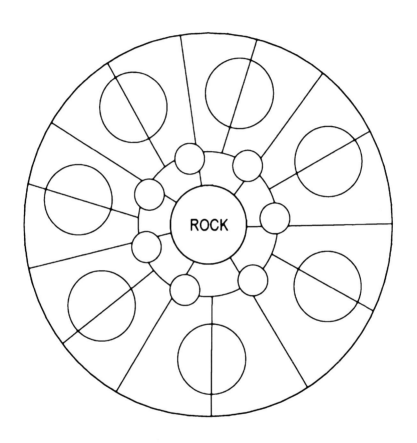

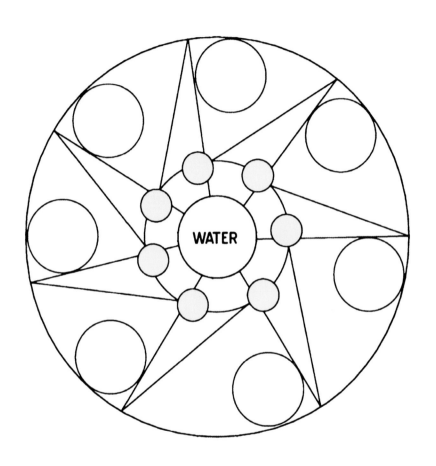

WATER

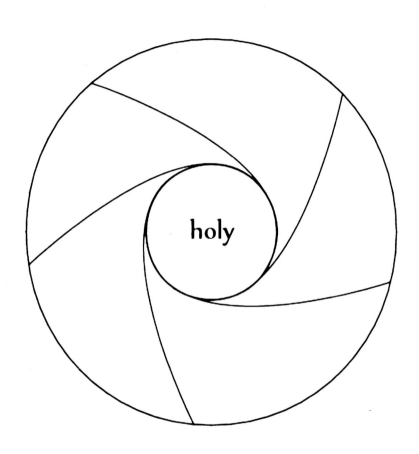

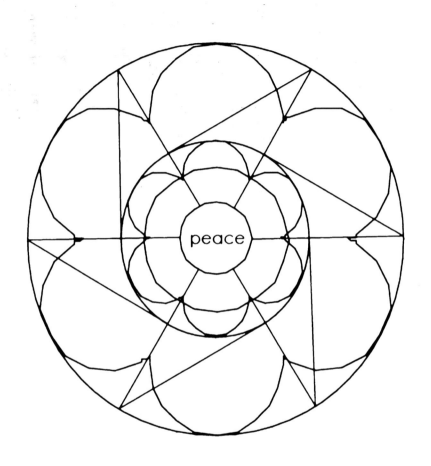

peace

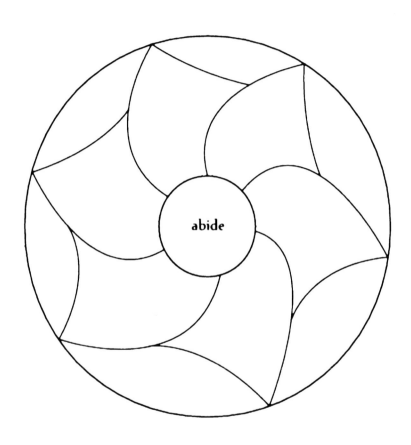

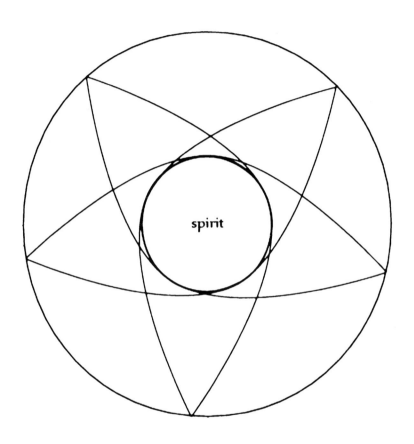

7
Faith Like a Child

Judged by the firm, settled, technical certitude of this age, or measured by the uncritical ideology of the world we take for granted, the world offered in the biblical tradition of poetic utterance hardly has a claim on reality. It so little fits the presumed world around us that the evangelical world of the tradition sounds like fiction. . . . It is precisely the daring work of fiction to probe beyond settled truth and to walk to the edge of alternatives not yet available to us.[14]

ONE REACTION TO CHANGE (whether in language or faith or life) is a hardening of orthodoxy, a determination that meanings must be finite, parameters fixed, and rules absolute. Change—especially quick or dramatic change—prompts us to long for answers, not questions. As life shifts, as language changes, as faith is challenged, we become tempted to view "truth" strictly as nonfiction, whether scientific fact or literal biblical interpretation or grammatical correctness. I'd like to check in on your experience of our retreat thus far: How are you experiencing change as we play with words and wonder over faith? Did we tiptoe too close to unorthodoxy for comfort as we imagined Jesus and the Spirit cruising in a Ford Mustang, or is the permission to explore faith freeing to your spirit? How are you reacting to the new perspectives on faith that we're engaging together in this sacred pause?

Thus far we've played with words, word sounds, word meanings, word mandalas. We haven't focused yet on the "why" of playing. Why do we play? Why do children play? What is gained, what is risked in playing? Do we "play" in faith—are we allowed to play in faith—and if so, how? When is the last time you played and laughed and let yourself be silly?

In general, playing lacks the requirement of a goal or final product. Time spent in play is often unstructured, and the only agendas are "fun" and "exploration." Play at its best gives us safe space to discover and test different perspectives. When kids play, for example, wooden blocks become buildings, a landscaping shrub becomes a forest, an empty box becomes a car or a cave. Kids see one object, but they have the imagination to see and engage the object as if it is something entirely different. Play provides a new perspective. Fundamentally, play recognizes the multiplicity of perspectives and, through curiosity and creativity, play tests out those other perspectives, those other truths.[15]

The playgrounds of the written word include fiction and myth and poetry. These literary genres toy with our perspectives by engaging our imaginations and creating a space in which we can see life afresh. Fiction, myth, and poetry invite us to ask that very childlike question—Why?—and by raising the question, these literary genres propose that we consider, even believe, improbable answers. Despite our very best efforts to grow up and to know everything and to have concrete answers, fiction prods us to grow young once again. As Jesus said to the crowd, "Truly I tell you, unless you change and become like children, you will never enter the kingdom of heaven" (Matt. 18:3). Fiction invites us to see that growing up into certainty may be the silliest venture of all.

"I don't believe I'll ever understand Grownups," said John. "They don't understand a single thing we say. But, worse than that, they don't understand what other things say. Why, only last Monday I heard Jane remark that she wished she knew the language the Wind spoke."

"They did once," said Mary Poppins, folding up one of Jane's nightgowns.

"What?" said John and Barbara together in very surprised voices. "Really? You mean they understood the Starling and the Wind and—"

"And what the trees say and the language of the sunlight and the stars—of course they did! Once," said Mary Poppins.

"But—but how is it that they've forgotten it all?" said John, wrinkling up his forehead and trying to understand.

"Because they've grown older," explained Mary Poppins.

"That's a silly reason," said John, looking sternly at her.[16]

Put on a childlike spirit for a moment and consider how very grown-up we tend to be in our faith. What are some of the biggest "grown-up" words in your faith vocabulary? What are some of the bulkiest words that you hear in church and read in the Bible? Which words do you use . . . and which ones do you avoid using? Of all those "grown-up" church words, which ones sound the funniest, and which words are awkward on our tongues? Words like:

Eschatology

Transubstantiation

Sacristy

Ecclesiastical

Acolyte

Beatitude

Canticle

Deuteronomy

Apse

Catechesis

Eucharist

Vestments

Pick one of these "serious" words and practice saying it aloud with great exaggeration, as we did in chapter 1. Can you make the word sound funny? Experiment with your vocal pitch and facial expressions as you repeat the word. Allowing our faith vocabulary to be funny, growing young again in wondering why we use such words, giving ourselves permission to remember that faith is not always solemn, can be a starting point for refreshing our spirits.

A favorite band of my college years, called The Woods Tea Company, has a great song that illuminates our silly habits with serious words: "Foolish Questions." The song pokes fun at the questions we often ask sincerely but without thinking.

> Now you've all heard foolish questions and you no doubt wonder why
> You know a person can ask a foolish question and expect a sensible reply

Like when you bring your girl some candy, say just
  after tea,
You know the first thing she's gonna do is wrinkle up
  her nose and ask,
"Is that for me?"
Foolish questions, why you may as well reply,
"No, that's for your ma and pa" or "I bought that for
  the guys."
"I just wanted you to look at it. Now I'm gonna take
  it away."
Foolish questions, you hear 'em every day.[17]

What "silly questions" would you like to ask about
faith and church? What questions do you suspect
people might like to ask but avoid (for example, "What
and where is the sacristy?")? Does it resonate with you
if I suggest that we occasionally hold back our questions
because we suspect that the answer is obvious and
that everyone else at church is "in the know"? In such
moments, the "foolishness" that holds us back is in fact
our self-consciousness and our fear of appearing unwise.
Foolish questions (whether actually foolish or merely
self-conscious), like fiction, can help us broaden our
perspective and engage that "whole world" of religious

words that we identified in chapter 6. Foolish questions can illuminate what is actual and what is assumed, what is playful and what is serious for us personally and within our faith traditions.

The key to foolish questions and fiction alike is childlike curiosity. Fostering such curiosity within ourselves is a necessary spiritual practice. It is the willingness to know how much we don't know . . . and simultaneously to believe far more than we deem certain or "factual." Curiosity must be nurtured, personally and interpersonally, in order for faith and for faith-in-community to grow. Christopher Johnson writes: "I believe that people could genuinely love language more if they shifted their focus from judgment and insecurity to curiosity and appreciation."[18] I believe the same about faith: that we can grow in love for God and one another when we value curiosity.

Let's play with questions and fiction in conjunction with Scripture. Let's ask silly, obvious questions, playful out-of-place questions, and then let's spin a few yarns of fiction. The lightheartedness of these exercises belies the purpose of helping us to hear familiar Bible teachings with new ears and to revalue a youthful heart in our spiritual lives. Curiosity and imagination are the purposes of this exercise, as we throw off the cloak of assumptions with which we approach Scripture and nurture a spirit of wonder in our reading.

To practice asking foolish questions of Bible verses, start with the basic question words: Who? What? When? Where? How? and that most notorious question that children ask, Why? On the following pages, I offer select verses for your curious questioning and sample questions to get you started. After adding your own questions, spend ten minutes (or more!) spinning a tale based on the verses, imagining a new storyline continuing in an entirely new direction from the given passage. It can be a challenge to be silly on our own; you may enjoy these exercises in a group, with trusted friends laughing together, compounding one another's silliness and venturing together with youthful frivolity.

And do not be afraid! Remember: it is God's foolishness that first imagined the laughable possibility of creation, of prophets speaking truth to power, of life after death. (To that end, another useful question to explore as you read is, Where is God's sense of humor in this passage?)

"The LORD is my shepherd, I shall not want."
(Ps. 23:1)

Why not? Why don't I want him?

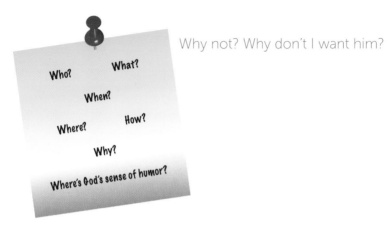

Fiction prompt (if you need one):
Imagine how it would look to have a shepherd
(and perhaps a few sheep) following you about
through your daily routine!

"Answer me when I call, O God of my right!"
(Ps. 4:1)

Are there roaming or long-distance charges in
heaven?

Fiction prompt (if you need one):
God takes control of your right hand . . .

*"On their hands they will bear you up,
so that you will not dash your feet against a stone."*
(LK. 4:11)

Who?   What?

When?

Where?   How?

Why?

Where's God's sense of humor?

Then why do I keep tripping?

Fiction prompt (if you need one):

You live your life walking just a few inches off
of the ground . . .

"I am about to do a new thing;
Now it springs forth, do you not perceive it?"
(Isa. 43:19)

How high can the new thing
bounce and spring?

Fiction prompt (if you need one):
A congregation goes on a scavenger hunt for
God's new thing . . .

"As Jesus walked by the Sea of Galilee, he saw two brothers, Simon, who is called Peter, and Andrew his brother, casting a net into the sea—
for they were fishermen."

(MATT. 4:18)

Who?   What?

When?

Where?   How?

Why?

Where's God's sense of humor?

Why else would they cast nets into the sea?

Fiction prompt (if you need one):
Peter and Andrew say "no" in response to Jesus' call . . .

8
Tipping Sacred Cows

We know nothing until we know
everything.

I have no object to defend
for all is of equal value
to me.

I cannot lose anything in this
place of abundance
I have found.

If something my heart cherishes
is taken away,

I just say, "Lord, what happened?"

And a hundred more appear.[19]

HEN A LOVED ONE DIES,
WE KNOW THAT TIME
FOR GRIEF IS NEEDED.

When we relocate between towns and jobs and schools, we anticipate a period of adjustment. Yet language changes almost daily, faith continually transforms, daily life hurtles forward at breakneck speed, and we barely pause to acknowledge the mind-body-soul impact that all of these daily changes have on us. Occasionally those changes demand space and recognition amid the whirlwind, as when a congregation debates the use of an inclusive hymnal for Sunday worship and time is needed for the congregation to grieve and reconcile the implications of such a change. Yet in large part, language shifts, faith develops, daily routines adapt, and we simply carry on.

The intentional acknowledgment of and reflection on the ever-changing landscape of language provide an opportunity not only to remember bygone words and welcome new ones but also to affirm the role of change in the life of faith. We may miss the twitter of birds now drowned out by the volume of Twitter, but ultimately—and this is important—in the abundance of the Word we cannot lose anything. In fact, the Word itself disrupts us, upends the familiar and the comfortable, in order to call us to fuller life.

What treasures, what habits of word and body and spirit, does the Word ask us to lose? The prophet Joel advises that we must be ready to drop everything for a new encounter with the Word. "Run away to God," he calls. "Leave what you are doing and hurry toward God! Gather all the people—bring your teachers and your infants, bring the couples from their wedding ceremonies, bring your siblings as well as the strangers among you. Declare a fast together so that you can pray to God without distraction! Interrupt your routine and run away to God who is gracious and merciful, slow to anger, and abounding in steadfast love" (Joel 2:12–16, adapted).

At God's beckon, would we disrupt our lives to the extent of leaving our own weddings? Would we interrupt our spending habits or walk away from our work schedules to answer the call to prayer? Would we lose a night of sleep to stay awake in waiting for God? Would we shed our worship traditions, explore new liturgical language, declare a fast from our theological arguments in order to receive the abundance of faith that is still to come? What are the extents and limits of disruption that we will risk in faith, for faith?

From our lives of flesh and breath, ashes and dust, from our own storerooms where we keep an excess of treasured routines, God calls us: "Run away to me! Come, hurry! Gather together and meditate on my goodness and mercy! Let me interrupt you so that I can satisfy you with a rich harvest of grace, an outpouring of joy, a touch of healing, a breath of fresh air. Let me interrupt you! Run away from those treasures that you thought would make life easier, from those golden calves that you hold onto for the sake of security, from the expectations that you have organized neatly on a shelf in your heart.

"Come! Run away to me, the Treasure of all treasures who does not trend out of style or grow dusty with tradition, the One who cannot be confined and who is not unsettled by change. Come, cherish the only and holy God!"

Psalm 46 echoes Joel's invitation to draw near to God during change, to hold fast to the One Who Is no matter what may be.

God is our shelter and strength; God remains
when all others flee in the face of trouble.
Therefore we will not fear, no matter the changes
in earth or heaven,

no matter the quaking of the mountains
or the foaming of the seas
or the roaring of the nations.
When God speaks, the earth cowers.
Change and trouble cannot overtake the God of
our ancestors.
Come, behold the One Who Is.
Be still and know that I am God.
(Ps. 46:1–4, 6–8, 10, adapted)

The Psalms are masterful in their ability to create prayerful space in which the changes of life can be acknowledged, the human condition expressed, and the blessing of God sought. The beauty of the Psalms is their ability to tell our present-day stories through ancient prayers. In the psalmist's quaking mountain, for example, you might hear echoes of your experience with a career change, while I might hear my story of a recent family death, and another reader might hear his or her fears of an actual earthquake. The Psalms adapt with each generation to narrate life in new ways—very much like *twitter* and *web* and *pop* and so many other words have developed new meanings for new generations. Amid constant change, then, the Psalms provide the opportunity not only to cherish what is familiar but also to explore what is new.

The following wordplay activity dives headfirst into change (and risks tipping a few sacred cows) by adapting beloved psalms through the style of MadLibs. (I call these MadLibbed psalms "LaudLibs.") Here we take advantage of the Psalms' flexibility in storytelling, trusting that what we lose in familiarity may nevertheless yield abundant new understanding. Lists are provided for you to brainstorm words before inserting them into the LaudLibs. Read each LaudLib aloud after filling in the blanks.

Use LaudLibs for devotions when your personal prayers are feeling stale, or create a congregational LaudLib during the "Children's Time" in worship. These LaudLibs are not intended to capture any one psalm exactly, but to find new joy and meaning (and a little spiritual silliness) in this creative wordplay.

LaudLib of Joy

positive describing word: _____

leader's title: _____

something that gives light: _____

planet name: _____

planet name: _____

small animal: _____

sea creature: _____

monster: _____

type of happy feeling: _____

type of dance: _____

LaudLib of Reassurance

something warm and fuzzy: _____

name of a superhero: _____

emotion: _____

emotion: _____

type of exercise: _____

something huge: _____

type of communication: _____

positive describing word: _____

LaudLib for Help

organ of the body: _____

gesture of greeting: _____

compliment: _____

positive characteristic: _____

task: _____

task: _____

famous scientist: _____

someone you admire:

historic figure: _____

organ of the body: _____

LaudLib of Humility

past-tense verb: _____

wrongdoing: _____

wrongdoing: _____

brand of detergent: _____

magic trick: _____

organ: _____

animal: _____

emotion: _____

emotion: _____

adjective: _____

LaudLib on Life

name for God: _____

type of dwelling: _____

type of geography: _____

famous building: _____

name of city: _____

name of city: _____

your age: _____

small animal: _____

large animal: _____

daily routine: _____

positive characteristic: _____

something really old: _____

continent: _____

type of disaster: _____

LaudLib of Thanks

an improvement: _____

item that brings you comfort: _____

method of travel: _____

action: _____

positive describing word: _____

positive describing word: _____

awesome animal: _____

impressive car: _____

award: _____

precious gem: _____

LaudLib of the Universe

bodies of water: _____

heavenly bodies: _____

something small in nature: _____

type of dance: _____

planet: _____

time of day: _____

time of day: _____

name for God: _____

synonym for roads: _____

name of a band: _____

type of artwork: _____

name of God: _____

LaudLib of Joy

God is _____! God is

(positive describing word)

_____ over the earth and the

(leader's title)

sea and the universe! God is like the biggest

_____, even brighter

(something that gives light)

than the stars and the sun! God knows

_____ and _____ .

(planet name)   *(planet name)*

God knows the _____ and the

(small animal)

_____; God even knows

(sea creature)

all about the _____! Be

(monster)

_____ that you know God! Do

(type of happy feeling)

the _____ to show your joy

(type of dance)

to God!

LaudLib of Reassurance

God is like a _____ when you
(something warm and fuzzy)

are afraid. God is like _____ when
(name of a superhero)

you are scared. God knows when you feel

_____ or _____. God
(emotion)   *(emotion)*

_____ with you every day. God is
(type of exercise)

like a _____ that cannot be moved,
(something huge)

so God will always be there! _____
(type of communication)

God anytime when you need someone to listen.

God is _____!
(positive describing word)

LaudLib for Help

Lend me your _____, God, (organ of the body)

because I need help. _____ at me (gesture of greeting)

when I cry out to you. You're _____ (compliment)

! You have so much _____! You (positive characteristic)

can do _____ and you can do (task)

_____, so I want you to be the (task)

one who helps me! I don't want to learn from

_____ or from _____ (famous scientist)   (someone you admire)

or even from _____; you're the (historic figure)

best teacher there is! I will study you with my

whole _____ forever! (organ of the body)

LaudLib of Humility

God, I've _____ a mess. Please
         (past-tense verb)

erase my _____ and forget about
         (wrongdoing)

my _____. Give me a bath in
      (wrongdoing)

_____. Like _____,
(brand of detergent)   *(magic trick)*

amaze me and help me see things differently.

You want my _____ to be
                  (organ)

naked to you and eager for wisdom. Let my

_____-ish soul dance with
      (animal)

_____ and _____, for
      (emotion)   *(emotion)*

you have put a _____ spirit in me!
                  (adjective)

LaudLib on Life

_____, you are a _____
(name for God)   you are a   *(type of dwelling)*

big enough for all people. You were our home

before humans lived on _____,
(type of geography)

before humans built _____, and
(famous building)

long before we lived in _____ or
(name of city)

_____. You are endless; I am only
(name of city)

_____. You see all of time like
(your age)

it's only a _____; I experience
(small animal)

one day like it's a _____. I change
(large animal)

my mind about _____ but your
(daily routine)

_____ doesn't change! Your love
(positive characteristic)

lasts longer than _____. Your wisdom
(something really old)

is bigger than _____. So even when
(continent)

_____ occurs, I will remember that
(type of disaster)

you alone are God.

LaudLib of Thanks

Thank you, God, for making me _____ !
(an improvement)

You are my _____. When I'm
(item that brings you comfort)

scared, I _____ to you and you
(method of travel)

help me. Now I'm going to _____
(action)

so people know that you're _____
(positive describing word)

and _____. If you were an animal,
(positive describing word)

you'd be a _____ because
(awesome animal)

you're amazing. If you were a car, you'd be

a _____ because you catch
(impressive car)

everyone's attention. But you're even better than

these: you're God! If I could, I would give you

the _____. You are more valuable
          (award)

to me than_____. Thank you, God,
              (precious gem)

for being you!

LaudLib of the Universe

There is a song being sung by _____
(bodies of water)

and _____. You can't hear it, but
(heavenly bodies)

even the _____ is singing
(something small in nature)

it. The song becomes a _____
(type of dance)

that _____ dances. The sun
(planet)

repeats the song at _____, and
(time of day)

the moon sings it at _____. This
(time of day)

is the song: "_____ is beautiful!
(name for God)

The _____ of God are good!"
(synonym for roads)

The trees clap, and the rain sings better

than _____, while God makes a
(name of a band)

_____ with the stars.
(type of artwork)

Who is God? _____ is! The whole
(name for God)

universe sings it!

9
In the Shadow of Wingdings

The poem is necessarily open-ended.
Its goal is not to tell a complete story, as a
novel does, but to use a life episode . . . to
inspire or even prod the reader to look at
life in a different way. Like Jesus' parables,
poems are usually considered unorthodox,
if not radical, precisely because they
challenge our usual and routine ways
of perceiving and construing our life
experiences, enticing us into viewing them
from a different angle or slant. [20]

F THE WORD MADE FLESH HAD INSTEAD
BECOME THE WORD MADE FONT,

I believe that the font most befitting such a miracle would be wingdings—bold, particular, geometric, captivating, and entirely puzzling. Wingdings is a graphic font that looks like an insolvable code. Those of us who bother with it learn several characters as needed—♌, ◆, ♒, ◻, ❖, and ◯ for example— but the entire wingdings "alphabet" is beyond memorization. We grasp bits and pieces but fail to acquire fluency in or make fullest use of wingdings as a format for communication. The symbols have little to no corporate meaning, unlike the symbols of our alphabet letters, which we commonly recognize by sight and sound. As visually engaging as it is, the wingdings font is nevertheless beyond understanding and ineffective for communication.

If anything remains with you from your retreat with this book, if anything continues to provoke your spirit, I hope it's the understanding that religious language is always and only an attempt to translate a Word that is beyond complete translation. Our words are an open-ended and imperfect attempt to express faith, much like poetry is an open-ended and never-ended observation of life. Just as alphabet letters capture the impression of vocal sounds, just as words strive to represent a picture of life experiences, our faith vocabulary is always striving yet never definitively articulating the meaning of the Word. We pause together for this creative retreat because we are aware of all that we do not know and all that language does not satisfactorily express.

Jesus told parables to express something beyond comprehension: the kingdom of God. His parables were winging stories, if you will; they were bold, particular, graphic, captivating, and entirely puzzling. As familiar as we may be with Jesus' parables, they continue to remind us that God's activities are beyond precise understanding. "What parable can we use for the mystery of God? What story can I tell to help you understand? It's like farming: the farmer scatters seeds on the ground and waters the field before going to bed. Day after day, the farmer watches the field through rain and sun, until suddenly the seeds sprout and become plants that grow tall in their rows: first the stalk, then the head, and finally the full grain. The farmer doesn't know quite how the seeds grow—it is a deep mystery, and yet it is basic to the farmer's life.

The farmer simply knows that when the field is fully grown and ripe, then it is time to harvest" (Mk. 4:26–29, adapted).

With many similar stories, Jesus spoke to the crowds and the disciples. Sometimes they understood his tales. Many times they did not. The stories were simple enough . . . but a parable or a poem or a wingding story cannot contain the mystery of God. After all, no eye has seen, no ear has heard, no human imagination has envisioned what God is able to do—what God is already doing—for the sake of the world that God loves (see 1 Cor. 2:9). As perplexing as the divine may be, however, that holy puzzle is also an invitation: to grow in spiritual imagination, to embrace the open-ended story that teaches us and unfolds within us, to find peace in the shadow of mysterious wingdings, even to tell our own adventures into unknown territories of faith. So we embrace the mysterious Word Made Font, and we tell our own parables of a God beyond imagining.

♏︎⌧︎♋︎⬥︎⬧︎♏︎♦ (a parable): The mystery of God at work in the world is like a kid in elementary school who is assigned to be the captain of a kickball team during gym class. The boy must build a winning kickball team by selecting his classmates in turns with the other team's captain. For his first pick, the boy chooses the least coordinated kid in class, the one with untied shoelaces and scrawny legs. From there, the captain continues to select the least popular, the least attractive, the least athletic kids to be the players on his kickball team.

This is the mystery of God's methods: that a prophet goes to a man named Jesse, looking for a king among Jesse's sons. The eldest and wisest son is presented first, but he is rejected. Likewise the second son who is tall and strong is passed by. And again the third son, whose face is handsome and his hair full of curls, is not considered for the throne. But the youngest son, hands still dirty from his work as a shepherd, face still sweaty because he has just run in from the fields, this one is chosen and anointed to be the next king of Israel.

We would do well to open our eyes.

ⅢⅩ☺○□●Ⅲ◆ (a parable): The mystery of God's Spirit at work in the world is like a grocery store that is filled with people even though its shelves are bare. You see, the people who shop at this grocery store bring groceries with them to the store: bags full of fresh produce and cereal boxes and gallons of milk and boxes of spaghetti and so much more. They fill shopping carts with the food that they've brought, and then they push those carts through the aisles of the grocery store, looking for other shoppers whose carts aren't as full or perhaps are empty, and they give their food away. There's no money exchanged, just food, here in this grocery store where the owner gives them a place to provide and share with friends, neighbors, and strangers alike.

This is the mystery of God's Spirit at work in the world: a church gathers for worship on Sunday, and many who come are spiritually overflowing from their own prayer lives and spiritual disciplines. They come to church for the opportunity to provide spiritual care and share the strength of community with those who are running on empty—both inside the church and outside of it. They come to church not to stuff themselves full of spiritual food, but to provide and share their spiritual resources with others who are hungry.

We would do well to open our hearts.

◻⌧♋○◻●♍✦ (a parable): What tale can I tell to hint at the expanse of God, to suggest the eternal possibilities for who God is and what God is doing, the possibilities beyond imagination for who we are and what God is calling us to do? What story can I tell to explain that mystery?

Does a mustard seed, the smallest of all seeds, not become the greatest of all shrubs, stretching out branches larger than the seed itself could have dared to imagine, branches large enough and leaves full enough to provide shelter and shade for many birds? And if the seed had remained tightly sealed in a seed packet, unopened, unplanted, how many birds could it have sheltered? How many nests could it have supported and covered with shade?

Does a business owner—just beginning her business and keenly aware of the debt that she has accumulated to open a new store—when she earns her first dollar from a customer, does she hurry to hide that dollar under a mattress, or does she frame the dollar and display it proudly in her store?

Does God hide from the world, too timid and overwhelmed by the state of affairs to engage in healing and loving and bringing justice? If God does not hide, are we truly so audacious and unmoved by the mystery and greatness of God that we would dare to hide away— unopened, unplanted—rather than risk loving, healing, speaking, seeking justice, extending grace, reconciling to one another in ways that we could not have imagined?

Our God is full of wingding stories. We would do well to open our ears.

In parables, in puzzling font, in poetry we strive to speak inconclusively and with ample room for mystery, in an effort to understand what escapes us. The experience of mystery that we practice most often in the life of faith is prayer. In our prayers, we brave communication with the Almighty Unknown. We pray with images and emotions, in our spirits and in our voices, sometimes without words and sometimes with recited words. In the language barrier between the Holy and the human, our prayers are wingdings striving for connection. "The Spirit helps us in our weakness; for we do not know how to pray as we ought, but that very Spirit intercedes with sighs too deep for words" (Rom. 8:26).

To step daringly into the space of prayer, to approach God with ample room for mystery, we occasionally must lay aside what we know: the routines of faith, the rubrics of communication, the formulas for prayer, the certitude of grammar structure, the rules of punctuation, even our certainties about God, so much of which we learned at a young age. I invite you into an open-ended and imaginative space of prayer. The following poem by Mary Oliver and Scripture prompts encourage you to pray in unfamiliar ways and without particular expectations, but simply with the willingness to sit in the shadows with the Mystery.

It doesn't have to be

the blue iris, it could be

weeds in a vacant lot, or a few

small stones; just

pay attention, then patch

a few words together and don't try

to make them elaborate, this isn't

a contest but a doorway

into thanks, and a silence in which

another voice may speak.[21]

"How long, O Lord? Will you forget me forever?"
(Ps. 13:1)

Write a list of questions—to God, about God, about life. Scatter the questions around this page. Do not write a "Dear God" or even an "Amen," only questions across the space.

> *"Those who wait for the LORD shall renew their strength,*
> *they shall mount up with wings like eagles."*
> (ISA. 40:31)

Write a prayer—whatever type of prayer you need today—only begin your writing at the bottom of the page and continue upward, so that your words rise and float as if on wings.

"My flesh and my heart may fail,
but God is the strength of my heart and my portion forever."
(Ps. 73:26)

Though flesh and breath and words may fail, still we continue to reach out to God in prayer. Let your words fall silent, and express a prayer using only emoticons.

> *"I will appoint Peace as your overseer*
> *and Righteousness as your taskmaster."*
> (Isa. 60:17)

Imagine if Peace was your overseer, your boss. Imagine if Righteousness wrote your "to do" list for you and commanded your daily tasks. Imagine if your energy and creativity—whether at work or at home or in the midst of errands—were directed by Justice, Compassion, and Grace. Write your day's "to do" list here; don't leave out any tasks: brewing coffee, stopping at the bank, sweeping the floor, and so on. After creating the list, overwrite each task with the word *PEACE* in bold black marker.

*"Justice will dwell in the wilderness
and righteousness abide in the fruitful field."*
(Isa. 32:16)

Sketch the landscape that you see outside
your window or perhaps a favorite skyline
that you recall in your mind's eye. Let the
exercise of drawing (regardless of precision or
skill) be a prayer for your environment.

"Holy Father, protect them in your name that you have given me, so that they may be one, as we are one."
(JOHN 17:11)

In a spirit of prayer, make a list of names. Do not write down or even dwell on your agenda to God for each person; simply write names as familiar faces come to mind. Write each name slowly, extending your heart as the ink extends across the paper.

10
Six Words,
140
Characters

Now—these few more words, and
   then I'm
gone: Tell everyone just to remember
their names, and remind others, later, when we
find each other. Tell the little ones
to cry and then go to sleep, curled up
where they can. And if any of us get lost,
remember: there will come a time when
all we have said and all we have hoped
will be all right.[22]

*I*N 2006, *SMITH* MAGAZINE BEGAN CURATING SIX-WORD AUTOBIOGRAPHIES, written by the famous, the infamous, and the unknown alike.

The project was fashioned after a six-word story purportedly written by Ernest Hemingway: "For sale: baby shoes, never worn."[23] The fullness of this story catches the heart and imagination with only six words. A story in six words, when whole novels and series of novels and thick tomes are written to tell stories. Yet in a rushed culture of headline skimming, Instagram snapshots, and 140-character Twitter bites, the power of a six-word story emphasizes that length of communication does not predetermine impact.

"God, grant me patience. Right now."—Michael Castleman[24]

"Learned. Forgot. Better off relearning anyway."—Brian DeLeeuw[25]

What makes six-word memoirs fascinating (and projects like it, such as Michele Norris's endeavor, "The Race Card Project"[26]) is not merely their brevity. "A successful [little] message sends people in the right direction but allows them to use their wits and the cues provided by context to get there. . . . A message starts a mental journey."[27] Brief messages intrigue us with what is left unsaid and the trail of connections (the networks and worlds from chapter 6) that the listener must follow.

Our words—and our faith—are not incapacitated by conciseness, whether constrained to six words or limited to 140 characters. To the contrary, we are enriched by the challenge to use language with reduced length and to express our faith with greater precision! Thus far in *Sacred Pause*, we have been expanding our understanding of words in order to expand our understandings of faith, magnifying and stretching the ways we look at and listen to words, swelling definition and detail, adding synonym and nuance and story until our words hold entire worlds. But the reality of our everyday use of words is that we cannot use the whole world of every word every time. For the sake of practicality, we survey the word choices before us (instantly, subconsciously), and we opt for the words best suited to a particular conversation or e-mail or prayer.

The challenge of brevity in communication and in faith is that we must be more deliberate in our word selection than we are accustomed to being. And we should be deliberate! In a world crowded by words, where every sound bite clamors for attention, we should absolutely practice care in every form of communication, because words have influence. Words can hinder or advance, promise or disappoint, encourage or condemn. In religious language, the careless word of a preacher can turn away a congregant, the lack of welcoming words at the church door can discourage a newcomer, a theological cliché in a moment of tragedy can encumber a person's faith. In both the religious and secular worlds, we are too accustomed to words that do not mean anything, that do not hold substance or integrity.

The prophet Micah slices right through the noise of disingenuous words in eighth-century-BCE in Jerusalem.

> Thus says the LORD concerning the prophets
>> who lead my people astray,
> who cry "Peace"
>> when they have something to eat,
> but declare war against those
>> who put nothing into their mouths.
> Therefore it shall be night to you, without vision,
>> and darkness to you, without revelation.
> The sun shall go down upon the prophets,
>> and the day shall be black over them;
> the seers shall be disgraced,
>> and the diviners put to shame;

they shall all cover their lips,

for there is no answer from God. (Mic. 3:5–7)

In other words, Micah declares: "Because you have been careless and deceitful with your words, there is now no Word. The Living Word is silent because you have neglected it and because you have spoken deceptively to the poorest and the most vulnerable among you.

"It is not enough," Micah says, "that your words say *Peace* while you wage new wars.

"It is not enough that your words say *Prosperity* while the hungry go unfed.

"It is not enough that your words say *All people* while you sit with rulers.

"It is not enough that your words promise *the brightest future* while your policies neglect the immediate needs of children and elderly alike.

"It is not enough that your words promise *security* while you abhor justice for the prisoner and decency for the noncitizen.

"You have abused your words and abused the least of these among you," says Micah. "Worst of all, you have abused your words in the name of *the* Word. You have lied to yourselves; you have convinced yourselves that the Living Word is still with you despite your neglect, convinced yourselves that the LORD God is present and that no harm will come to you because corrupt priests and prophets have prayed, 'God bless us.'

"But there will be no Word from God as long as you spew self-righteous words, as long as you continue such disgraceful work. Alas for those who perform evil deeds simply because it is within their power!"

We have been playing with words and with the Word in the luxury of a retreat atmosphere, soothing ourselves with the pleasure and creativity of words, but as we lift our eyes from the pages of this book to examine our lives and reflect on our world, we must consider: where is *the Word* in these days so full of useless and abusive words?

Because God is connected to tangible life, because the Word labored to call the world into tangible being, because we are connected and called to love one another, any Word that professes to be good news must be connected to the work of genuine life-giving relationships. Any Word that declares itself to be authoritative must be connected to the tangible work of reconciling community. We who stake our Christian worldview on the belief that the Word became flesh must ask, Do our words have flesh? Are we connecting our words to our lives? Are we connecting our lives to *the* Word? Are we reciting the Word, or are we involved in the Word? How are we living out the faith that we talk about?

Micah cuts away all that is extra, every excess that we wrap around us, and asks that most familiar question:

> What does the LORD require of you
> but to do justice, and to love kindness,
>> and to walk humbly with your God? (Mic. 6:8)

Micah pierces through the words of war jargon, of vain religious ritual, and of political posturing with a six-word message: "Do justice. Love kindness. Walk humbly."

Whether in six words or in sixty, in 140 characters or in 14,000 characters, our words should demonstrate our embodied faith with integrity and congruity. And if we dare to take the challenge of brevity, then we have the opportunity—like Micah—to cut through the words that inundate our senses in order to see and hear and share what is essential: a core message of good news that captures our hearts and engages our imaginations. To return to the poem that opened this chapter, for example, William Stafford's "few more words" might be condensed into this six-word lesson: "Remember your name. Find each other." In other words, do not forget who you are and Whose you are; do not neglect to connect with one another, no matter the chaos.

Practice discerning a core message of good news or a life lesson for each of the following Gospel readings. Read the passage several times. Pay attention to its emotion as well as its content. Listen for how the passage resonates with your spirit. If the reading is familiar, try to hear what you may not have heard before; read the passage aloud to help you listen. Finally, write the message that your soul hears. Use your own words. You may need to start with a longer draft and edit the message down to six words. You might find yourself discerning multiple messages and lessons from any given passage, and thus writing multiple six-word messages. As you write, rest assured that there are not "right" and "wrong" answers, only the opportunity to hear God afresh.

Just then some men came, carrying a paralyzed man on a bed. They were trying to bring him in and lay him before Jesus; but finding no way to bring him in because of the crowd, they went up on the roof and let him down with his bed through the tiles into the middle of the crowd in front of Jesus. When he saw their faith, he said, "Friend, your sins are forgiven you." Then the scribes and the Pharisees began to question, "Who is this who is speaking blasphemies? Who can forgive sins but God alone?" When Jesus perceived their questionings, he answered them, "Why do you raise such questions in your hearts? Which is easier, to say, 'Your sins are forgiven you,' or to say, 'Stand up and walk'? But so that you may know that the Son of Man has authority on earth to forgive sins"—he said to the one who was paralyzed—"I say to you, stand up and take your bed and go to your home." Immediately he stood up before them, took what he had been lying on, and went to his home, glorifying God." (Lk. 5:18–25)

Again Jesus spoke to them, saying, "I am the light of the world. Whoever follows me will never walk in darkness but will have the light of life." Then the Pharisees said to him, "You are testifying on your own behalf; your testimony is not valid." Jesus answered, "Even if I testify on my own behalf, my testimony is valid because I know where I have come from and where I am going, but you do not know where I come from or where I am going. You judge by human standards; I judge no one. Yet even if I do judge, my judgment is valid; for it is not I alone who judge, but I and the Father who sent me. In your law it is written that the testimony of two witnesses is valid. I testify on my own behalf, and the Father who sent me testifies on my behalf." Then they said to him, "Where is your Father?" Jesus answered, "You know neither me nor my Father. If you knew me, you would know my Father also." (John 8:12–19)

He left that place and entered their synagogue; a man was there with a withered hand, and they asked him, "Is it lawful to cure on the sabbath?" so that they might accuse him. He said to them, "Suppose one of you has only one sheep and it falls into a pit on the sabbath; will you not lay hold of it and lift it out? How much more valuable is a human being than a sheep! So it is lawful to do good on the sabbath." Then he said to the man, "Stretch out your hand." He stretched it out, and it was restored, as sound as the other. (Matt. 12:9–13)

As he was walking along, he saw Levi son of Alphaeus sitting at the tax booth, and he said to him, "Follow me." And he got up and followed him.

And as he sat at dinner in Levi's house, many tax collectors and sinners were also sitting with Jesus and his disciples—for there were many who followed him. When the scribes of the Pharisees saw that he was eating with sinners and tax collectors, they said to his disciples, "Why does he eat with tax collectors and sinners?" When Jesus heard this, he said to them, "Those who are well have no need of a physician, but those who are sick; I have come to call not the righteous but sinners." (Mk. 2:14–17)

A certain ruler asked him, "Good Teacher, what must I do to inherit eternal life?" Jesus said to him, "Why do you call me good? No one is good but God alone. You know the commandments: 'You shall not commit adultery; You shall not murder; You shall not steal; You shall not bear false witness; Honor your father and mother.'" He replied, "I have kept all these since my youth." When Jesus heard this, he said to him, "There is still one thing lacking. Sell all that you own and distribute the money to the poor, and you will have treasure in heaven; then come, follow me." (Lk. 18:18–22)

11
The Seventh Day

Loving God is like loving silent
movies. There are kaleidoscopes
of colorful emotion, juggernauts of
reeling action, autographs of written text,
and narrative schemes of implied ethical
direction. But there is no sound. Yes, there
is voice; every story, every power has a
voice, a way of viewing the world and being
viewed by it, that signals a message as
much by how it "speaks" as by what it "says."
Voice, though, does not require sound.
It needs only an audience and a channel
to reach it. The physical ear need not be
involved.[28]

THE WORD THAT HAS BEEN FROM THE
BEGINNING OFTEN "SPEAKS" IN SILENCE.

To Elijah after the mountain's roaring tumult (1 Kgs. 19). Like a dream in the night to Eliphaz (Job 4). As a holy calm against all storms (Ps. 65). Through the muted voice of Zechariah (Lk. 1). The Word seeks out the silent spaces in our lives, cracks open a new space if needed, to whisper into the ear of the soul. The Word makes use of silence to communicate . . . as do our words. Without space and silence, how would we discern the end of a sentence or story? Without space and silence, how would we have a conversation or hear the rhythm of a poem or read between the lines for subtext? Without space and silence, how would we recognize the end of one word and the beginning of the next?

Imagine if words and sounds did not include silence and space! HowwouldwedistinguishthoughtandconnectioninconversationwitheachotherletalonewithGod? Without space in which to arrange and understand words, without silence to separate phrases and allow ideas to flow, how would we build relationships or learn from one another or be inspired? How, for example, would we make sense of Paul's soaring (and lengthy) rhetorical letters without silence?

WhenGodwhohadsetmeapartbeforeIwasbor
nandcalledmethroughhisgracewaspleasedtorev
ealhisSontomesothatImightproclaimhimamon
gtheGentilesIdidnotconferwithanyhumanbe
ingnordidIgouptoJerusalemtothosewhowereal
readyapostlesbeforemebutIwentawayatonceto
ArabiaandafterwardsIreturnedtoDamascus.(Gal.
1:15–17)

Silence and space shape language just as much as vowels and consonants do—and goodness knows, Paul's writing needs the help of space for comprehension.

> When God
> *which God? the one who had set me apart before I*
> *   was born and called me through his grace*
> was pleased to reveal his Son to me
> *for what purpose? so that I might proclaim him*
> *   among the Gentiles,*
> I did not confer with any human being
> *no one at all? not even those in Jerusalem who were*
> *   already apostles before me*
> but I went away at once into Arabia
> *that is, I took time and space for silence*
> and afterwards I returned to Damascus.

We properly steward words when we attend to their need for silence, in speech and in print. We rightly honor the Word when we practice Sabbath in our communication and in our lives. The model for a Sabbath of words was given by the Word itself.

"In the beginning was the Word, and the Word was with God, and the Word was God. He was in the beginning with God. All things came into being through him, and without him not one thing came into being. What came into being in him was life, and light.

"What came into being in him was a light to govern the day and a lesser light to travel through the night. What came into being through the Word was a dome that was called the sky and waters that gathered together into seas and dry places that were the earth. What came into being through the Word was vegetation, and fruit, and stars, and seasons, and birds in the air, and monsters in the seas, and beasts on the land, and humankind crafted in the image of God. What came into being through the Word was the breath of life shared by every plant-yielding seed, by every beast in cave and tree and field, by every bird warming its nest, by every creeping thing sneaking low to the earth.

"What came into being through the Word in the beginning was all good, very good. What came into being through the Word was life and light. And when the beginning of all life was completed, when the task of creating life was fully initiated, then the Word rested. And the rest was blessed and made holy."[29]

The Word rested and consecrated rest as a necessary element of creativity, of love, of life. The Word required rest . . . and our words require rest! Our words require space and silence. We who talk all day, text and e-mail and blog, read and listen and talk some more, we need silence in our words and silence in our souls in order to be rejuvenated just as the words themselves need silence in order to be utilized.

Ironically perhaps, we take for granted the necessity of silence in our language while we resist its importance in our faith. When was the last time you stopped, made space for silence in your life? I don't mean "slowed down." I don't mean "found a better balance between work and recreation." I don't mean "read the newspaper while savoring a cup of coffee." I mean "stopped."

When is the last time you came to a complete stop in activity and in spirit, placed a period at the end of this run-on sentence you're pushing yourself to live?

We need to stop occasionally. We need to step away from people—all people, even family and best friends. We need to leave our schedules and "to do" lists. We need to put everything down and simply be. Even ten minutes of stopping every day—breathing and listening to God's silent voice in the expanse of space—can be the Sabbath that is needed to sustain our souls. Remember: even when the Word lived in flesh and crammed the fullness of God's love into the limits of human life, even then Jesus practiced space and silence. Even when a day was crammed with teaching in the synagogue and healing a man with unclean spirits and reviving Peter's mother-in-law and curing a whole city's ailing citizens, even then Jesus cracked open space in his life to stop. "In the morning, while it was still very dark, he got up and went out to a deserted place, and there he prayed" (Mk. 1:35).

Even if it means getting up before the sun rises, even if it means retreating from very important work, we must stop   and take space and be silent. Where do you have space (or where can you create space) that is silent? Perhaps not void of all sound, but void of external distractions. Space where your spirit can listen beyond its inner distractions. Space where your spirit can tune its ear to the Word that comes in silence, saying:

Listen.

Listen.

Sit. And breathe. And listen.

There is no rush.

No need to hurry through this quiet moment.

My work is always there to be done,
your work is always there to be done,
but for now all work must wait.

Do not even try to put words to prayer.
Just ssshh.

Breathe.

Rest.

Listen.

You have been mine from the very first.

The world cannot take my love from you
(though you may forget if you do not stop to
remember).

You have been consecrated, you have been blessed.
Just look and see how far you've come.
See how I've guarded you, see how I've taught you.

Take a deep breath.

Nestle into your prayers with me.
No need to barter for blessings;
you are abundantly blessed in this time

and in this silence.

This is not a time for providing answers or solving puzzles.

This is a time for simply sitting with me.

Sssshhh.

I love you.

That is enough.

12
How Beautiful the Word

If Jesus were fully human and only seemingly divine, that would be of no help to us, for there would be nothing in him to lift us above what keeps us low and compromised. . . . If Christ Jesus is truly God, but only seemingly human . . . then we are left still godless in our sins and successes, our joys and sorrows, our laughter and our tears. . . . If, however, God joins us in this "vulnerable flesh to place his Father's kiss upon our faces," if, in fact, Jesus really is one of us, a down-to-earth man among us women and men, then everything is changed. We are not alone.[30]

IT MATTERS THAT THE DIVINE WORD TOOK ON THE BLOOD AND BREATH OF HUMAN LIFE.

It matters that the Word wrapped itself in sound and space, motion and emotion, action and language, routine and relationships. The enfleshed Word makes a difference to our own sound and space, motion and emotion, action and language, routine and relationships. When we play with words for spiritual enrichment, our purpose is not mere entertainment but the transformation of our lives in response to a Word that matters.

As this creative retreat concludes—or, more appropriately, as it continues beyond the bindings of this book—we commit our lives and our words to transformation by Christ. In the following spaces, write prayers of dedication for the words that you use every day and for the circumstances of those words. The prompt for each prayer adopts the words of Psalm 103:1:

> Bless the LORD, O my soul,
> and all that is within me,
> bless his holy name.

Bless the Word, O my e-mailed words, and all that is within me, bless God's holy name.

Bless the Word, O my words sung loudly in the car, in the shower, in the church, and all that is within me, bless God's holy name.

Bless the Word, O my words spoken to family, and all that is within me, bless God's holy name.

Bless the Word, O my Facebook words, and all that is within me, bless God's holy name.

B less the Word, O my words of work, and all that is within me, bless God's holy name.

B less the Word, O my tweeted words, and all that is within me, bless God's holy name.

Bless the Word, O my prayed words, and all
that is within me, bless God's holy name.

Bless the Word, O my listening spirit, and all
that is within me, bless God's holy name.

The Word that transforms us became flesh for us and lived among us, glorious like a light shining through the deepest night. How beautiful the Word that took on flesh and breath! How beautiful the Word that took on family and friends, the Word that became an infant . . . a toddler . . . a young man . . . a teacher . . . the Word that walked among us, touched us, loved us. How beautiful is the Word that loves us still.

How beautiful is the blazing Word as it signals hope: hope in the midst of loneliness, hope for the impossible overturning of oppression and hunger and poverty, hope that this is not it—that this is not all—and death is not the final word. How sweet it is to our souls that the Word of hope comes to the smallest, the weakest, the oldest, the poorest, the hidden, the lost, and the overlooked, as an unexpected refrain.

How beautiful is the surprising Word that brings peace like a child leading lions, lambs, and asps together. How delightful, how longed-for! How beautiful the words of the messengers who announce and embody peace: peace to the beggar waiting at the city gate, peace to the lepers cast out of their own families, peace to the woman no one will touch, and peace to the woman who is beaten. Peace in a time of corruption and hatred and violence and fear.

How beautiful—oh, how needed!—is the prophetic Living Word that brings joy, that begins joy, even amid a dry desert, even amid economic worries and church politics and family strain and hearts desperate for wholeness! How splendid the good news of joy that is for all people. How beautiful the Holy Word of joy that is embodied in e-mail and prayer, in sermon and church newsletter, in tweet and conversation, in word and in silence.

How beautiful is the Holy Word of love that continues, the Holy Love that still lives and most surely still acts! How beautiful the Word Made Flesh that embodies love for all people, in all places: love for you, for me; love for the estranged and love for the lovers; love for the refugee, the stranger, the outcast. Love so holy and so vast and so unconditional that we can only imagine the tip of the iceberg that is the depth of Love, we can only write poetry and tell tall tales to hint at its brilliant mystery!

How beautiful across the church and around the world are the words of those who are transformed by the Word, the messengers who practice peace, who demonstrate good news, who work for healing, who proclaim in hope, "Your God reigns." How beautiful is the Word that delights the discouraged, the Word that quickens healing, the Word that is our life.

> How beautiful upon the mountains
> > are the feet of the messenger who announces
> > > peace,
> who brings good news,
> > who announces salvation,
> > who says to Zion, "Your God reigns."
> > > (Isa. 52:7)

In the beginning was the Word, and the Word was with God, and the Word was God. And the Word was beautiful! The Word became flesh and lived among us in all its beauty, and we have seen its glory. In the Word was life, and the life was the light of all people. The light of the Word shines in the darkness, and the darkness does not overcome it. And the people of the Word are forever called to speak it, to sing it, to write it, to pray it, so that the light and the life which are the Word will continue to heal the world, will continue to redefine love in abundance for all people.

How beautiful the Word! How blessed, how very blessed are we to be its messengers!

My words are like tongs
handling the hazy red coals
of a fire too holy
which nevertheless
has called me to its side.
So I whisper: "Beautiful!"
and an ember pulses brighter;
"Delightful!" and a spark
cracks with laughter;
"Restorative!" and
a flame licks warmly.
"You are unchanging and
ever-surprising," I woo,
and the fire swells.
"You are satisfying and
unsettling," I affirm,
and then I set the tongs down
while I bask on the hearth
and rebuild my courage
for handling the fire again.

NOTES

1 Christopher Johnson, *Microstyle: The Art of Writing Little* (New York: W. W. Norton, 2011), 12.

2 Ibid., 119.

3 Robert Beckford, *Jesus Dub: Theology, Music and Social Change* (London: Routledge, 2006), 26.

4 Charles L. Bartow, *God's Human Speech: A Practical Theology of Proclamation* (Grand Rapids: Eerdmans, 1997), 73.

5 Johnson, *Microstyle*, 129.

6 Bartow, *God's Human Speech*, 63–64.

7 Simone Weil, as quoted in *For Lovers of God Everywhere: Poems of the Christian Mystics*, ed. Roger Housden (Carlsbad, CA: Hay House, 2009), 148.

8 Johnson, *Microstyle*, 18–19.

9 John Langdon, *Wordplay: The Philosophy, Art, and Science of Ambigrams* (New York: Broadway, 2005), 156.

10 Johnson, *Microstyle*, 37.

11 Albert-László Barabási, *Linked: How Everything Is Connected to Everything Else and What It Means for Business, Science, and Everyday Life* (New York: Plume, 2003), 19.

12 Langdon, *Wordplay*, 11.

13 Ibid., 11–15.

14 Walter Brueggemann, *Finally Comes the Poet: Daring Speech for Proclamation* (Minneapolis: Fortress, 1989), 5.

15 Langdon, *Wordplay*, 32–40.

16 P. L. Travers, *Mary Poppins and Mary Poppins Comes Back* (New York: Harcourt, Brace & World, 1963), 92–94.

17 The Woods Tea Company, "Foolish Questions," *The Wood's Tea Co. – Live! Collector's Edition* (1999).

18 Johnson, *Microstyle*, 12.

19 Catherine of Siena, as quoted in *For Lovers of God Everywhere*, 124.

20 Donald Capps, *The Poet's Gift: Toward the Renewal of Pastoral Care* (Louisville: Westminster John Knox Press, 1993), 2.

21 Mary Oliver, "Praying" from *Thirst* (Boston: Beacon Press, 2006), 37.

22 William Stafford, quoted in Donald Capps, *The Poet's Gift*, 34.

23 *Smith* magazine, ed., *Not Quite What I Was Planning: Six-Word Memoirs by Writers Famous and Obscure* (New York: HarperCollins, 2008), v.

24 Ibid., 132.

25 Ibid., 151.

26 http://theracecardproject.com.

27 Johnson, *Microstyle*, 34.

28 Brian K. Blount, *Then the Whisper Put on Flesh: New Testament Ethics in an African American Context* (Nashville: Abingdon, 2001), 13.

29 Adapted from Gen. 1–2 and John 1.

30 Bartow, *God's Human Speech*, 14–15.

31 The quoted text ("vulnerable flesh to place his Father's kiss upon our faces") is from William Brower's unpublished poem, "Advent."

ACKNOWLEDGMENTS AND THANKS

I am grateful to and greatly informed by the work of Christopher Johnson in *Microstyle* (New York: W. W. Norton, 2011). My writing personally and professionally is prompted often by Judy Reeves's *A Writer's Book of Days* (Novato, CA: New World Library, 1999). The ever-wonderful RevGalBlogPals provided the first opportunity for me to employ this material during their continuing education Big Event in 2013, and I am continually blessed to participate in the RGBP network.

ABOUT PARACLETE PRESS

Paraclete Press is a publisher of books, recordings, and DVDs on Christian spirituality. Our publishing represents a full expression of Christian belief and practice—from Catholic to Evangelical, from Protestant to Orthodox.

We are the publishing arm of the Community of Jesus, an ecumenical monastic community in the Benedictine tradition. As such, we are uniquely positioned in the marketplace without connection to a large corporation and with informal relationships to many branches and denominations of faith.

WHAT WE ARE DOING

Paraclete Press Books | Paraclete publishes books that show the richness and depth of what it means to be Christian. Although Benedictine spirituality is at the heart of all that we do, we publish books that reflect the Christian experience across many cultures, time periods, and houses of worship. We publish books that nourish the vibrant life of the church and its people.

We have several different series, including the best-selling Paraclete Essentials and Paraclete Giants series of classic texts in contemporary English; Voices from the Monastery—men and women monastics writing about living a spiritual life today; award-winning poetry; best-selling gift books for children on the occasions of baptism and first communion; and the Active Prayer Series that brings creativity and liveliness to any life of prayer.

Mount Tabor Books | Paraclete's newest series, Mount Tabor Books, focuses on liturgical worship, art and art history, ecumenism, and the first millennium church; and was created in conjunction with the Mount Tabor Ecumenical Centre for Art and Spirituality in Barga, Italy.

Paraclete Recordings | From Gregorian chant to contemporary American choral works, our recordings celebrate the best of sacred choral music composed through the centuries that create a space for heaven and earth to intersect. Paraclete Recordings is the record label representing the internationally acclaimed choir Gloriæ Dei Cantores, praised for their "rapt and fathomless spiritual intensity" by *American Record Guide*; the Gloriæ Dei Cantores Schola, specializing in the study and performance of Gregorian chant; and the other instrumental artists of the Gloriæ Dei Artes Foundation.

Paraclete Press is also privileged to be the exclusive North American distributor of the recordings of the Monastic Choir of St. Peter's Abbey in Solesmes, France, long considered to be a leading authority on Gregorian chant.

Paraclete Video | Our DVDs offer spiritual help, healing, and biblical guidance for a broad range of life issues including grief and loss, marriage, forgiveness, facing death, bullying, addictions, Alzheimer's, and spiritual formation.

Learn more about us at our website: www.paracletepress.com or phone us toll-free at 1.800.451.5006

SCAN TO READ MORE

ALSO BY RACHEL HACKENBERG

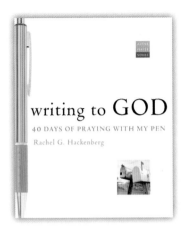

Writing to God
40 Days of Praying with My Pen

ISBN: 978-1-55725-879-3 | $15.99, Paperback

If you love to write, or if you need to spark your creativity, this book is for you. *Writing to God* offers forty insightful days of prayer and personal reflection with poems and thoughts to prompt your own prayers.

"Praying by writing takes a prayer out of my head
and makes praying a whole-body exercise: my creativity is
sparked, my spirit fully focused, my muscles employed, my
sense of touch and awareness of breath heightened.
I felt more connected to prayer than I had ever
experienced before." —Rachel Hackenberg

Writing to God
Kids' Edition

ISBN: 978-1-61261-107-5 | $12.99, Paperback

Writing to God: Kids' Edition offers guidance to kids that
parents can also appreciate: It teaches them how to pray to
God creatively through their pens (or pencils, or crayons).

In 35 days, kids learn how to pray to God using their
senses, reflecting on their feelings, in light of Bible verses,
looking at nature, to understand the ordinary events of life,
to use new words and pictures for God, and writing to God
as a way to say "thank you."

Available from most booksellers or through Paraclete Press:
www.paracletepress.com
1-800-451-5006
Try your local bookstore first.